Index

Deal 1

A Small (or Little, or Mini) Slam is a 12 trick contract - "Six of Something". On about one deal in 15 a Small Slam can be made. A bonus of 500 points is given for a successful Small Slam when non-vulnerable (no game yet scored); and a bonus of 750 points is given for a successful slam when vulnerable.

However a failing Small Slam venture means that no points at all are scored, the opponents scoring penalty points for the failure (in the normal fashion - 50 points for each undertrick non-vulnerable and 100 for each undertrick vulnerable).

As a rough guide, a Small Slam is worth attempting if it is better than an even-money proposition.

A Grand Slam is a 13 trick contract - "Seven of Something". Unable to afford to lose a single trick, these are much harder to make and, in spite of their obvious lure, should only rarely be attempted.

A non-vulnerable Grand Slam scores a bonus of 1000 points, and a vulnerable Grand Slam scores a wapping 1500 point bonus. But a failure scores no points at all (the opponents scoring the penalty points). Thus a Grand Slam failing by one trick is a massive wasted opportunity (with a Small Slam available).

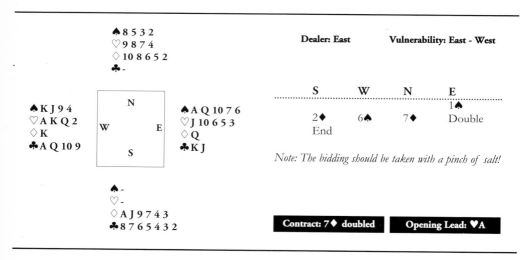

Dealer: East   Vulnerability: East - West

S	W	N	E
			1♠
2♦	6♠	7♦	Double
End			

Note: The bidding should be taken with a pinch of salt!

Contract: 7♦ doubled	Opening Lead: ♥A

Having warned of the risks of bidding for all 13 tricks, I cannot resist showing you a Grand Slam deal with just five high-card points (the lowest amount possible).

In 7♦ doubled, declarer trumped West's ace of hearts lead, trumped a club, crossed back to the ace of trumps (felling the king and queen), trumped a second club, trumped a spade (or heart), trumped a third club, trumped a spade, trumped a fourth club, trumped another spade, then tabled his last four cards: three established clubs and the last trump.

Grand Slam made!

Deal 2

Last page we saw declarer make a Grand Slam with just five high-card points. It was an extreme example, but it highlighted an important point: that many tricks can be made without honours - using trumps and long suit(s).

However I am sure you would agree that it is hard enough making all 13 tricks on a hand, let alone bidding for them. So from now on we will concentrate on Small Slams - and if I use the casual term "slam" I can be assumed to be referring to a Small Slam not a Grand Slam.

When there is no particular trump fit, no long suit and relatively balanced hands, the temptation will be to try for a Notrump slam. It should be borne in mind, however, that the advantage of a Notrump game, that fewer tricks than trump games are needed, does not hold for slams. 12 tricks are needed for all slams.

Notrump slams require many high-card points - 33 out of the 40 available to be precise (and this proves to be an accurate guideline). One way of remembering this number is that it is the fewest number of points where it is impossible for the opponents to hold two aces.

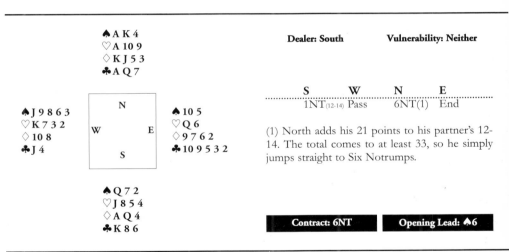

♠ A K 4
♡ A 10 9
◇ K J 5 3
♣ A Q 7

♠ J 9 8 6 3
♡ K 7 3 2
◇ 10 8
♣ J 4

♠ 10 5
♡ Q 6
◇ 9 7 6 2
♣ 10 9 5 3 2

♠ Q 7 2
♡ J 8 5 4
◇ A Q 4
♣ K 8 6

Dealer: South **Vulnerability: Neither**

S	W	N	E
1NT(12-14)	Pass	6NT(1)	End

(1) North adds his 21 points to his partner's 12-14. The total comes to at least 33, so he simply jumps straight to Six Notrumps.

Contract: 6NT **Opening Lead: ♠6**

Our second deal deal saw North correctly jump from 1NT to 6NT (33 points held), and West led the six of spades. Counting 11 top tricks (three spades, one heart, four diamonds and three clubs), he needed just one more. This could only come from the heart suit, using finessing technique.

Declarer won the queen of spades and immediately led a low heart to dummy's nine. East won the queen and returned a second spade to dummy's king. Crossing to his ace of diamonds, declarer then led a second heart to dummy's ten. With West holding the king, dummy's ten scored the trick (the crucial extra trick). Declarer cashed the ace of hearts and the ace of spades, crossed to the queen of diamonds, returned to dummy's king-jack, then took the last three tricks with the three top clubs.

Slam made.

Deal 3

Tricks are made in three ways: with high-cards; with trumps; and with long suits. Because Notrump Slams cannot use trumps, nor do they generally contain much in the way of length (or the long suit would be trumps), they need many high-card points - 33 to be precise - for success to be likely.

On hearing his partner open 1NT, North's first reaction was to go slamming. But even 3NT was a tricky contract when West hit declarer's weak spot - spades - his lead of the six going to East's queen.

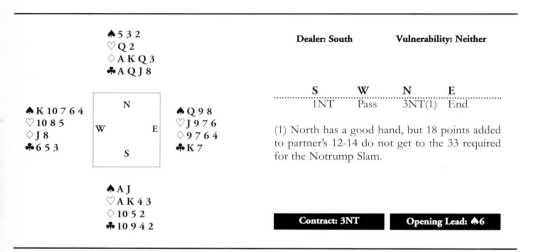

		♠ 5 3 2			
		♡ Q 2			
		◇ A K Q 3			
		♣ A Q J 8			

Dealer: South **Vulnerability: Neither**

	S	W	N	E
	1NT	Pass	3NT(1)	End

♠ K 10 7 6 4   ♠ Q 9 8
♡ 10 8 5   ♡ J 9 7 6
◇ J 8   ◇ 9 7 6 4
♣ 6 5 3   ♣ K 7

(1) North has a good hand, but 18 points added to partner's 12-14 do not get to the 33 required for the Notrump Slam.

♠ A J
♡ A K 4 3
◇ 10 5 2
♣ 10 9 4 2

Contract: 3NT   **Opening Lead: ♠6**

Declarer counted eight top tricks - one spade, three hearts, three diamonds and one club. One more needed.

Declarer ducked East's queen of spades, and won his continuation of the nine. How should he try to make his extra trick?

Here is the trap: do not take the club finesse yet (running the ten). If it loses (to East's king), the defence are likely to defeat the contract with three more spade winners (they would).

The correct suit to broach first is diamonds. Cross to dummy's ace-king at Tricks Three and Four. In fact West's jack falls on the second round, so return to the ten (the extra trick), lead back to dummy's queen of hearts, cash the queen of diamonds, return to the ace-king of hearts and finally lead to the ace of clubs (the ninth trick).

Had the jack of diamonds not fallen in two rounds, continue with the queen of diamonds, hoping for a 3-3 split (in which case dummy's three will be a length winner). If the suit fails to split 3-3, the club finesse must be taken (leading dummy's queen of hearts, crossing to the ace-king, then running the ten of clubs).

The key point is that the club finesse should be a last resort because if it fails, the lead is lost, and with it the contract.

Deal 4

We have ascertained that a Notrump (Small) Slam requires 33 points. If you are happy to play Notrumps rather than in a suit, then count the total number of points held by the partnership.

If there are definitely 37 or more points (rare), bid 7NT. If there are definitely 33 or more points, bid 6NT. If there are definitely fewer than 33 points, settle for 3NT.

But what if there may be 33 points (if partner is maximum), but there may not (if he is minimum)?

The answer is to go beyond game, thus announcing slam intentions, but not by more than one level, enabling partner to pass with a minimum hand. Bid 4NT.

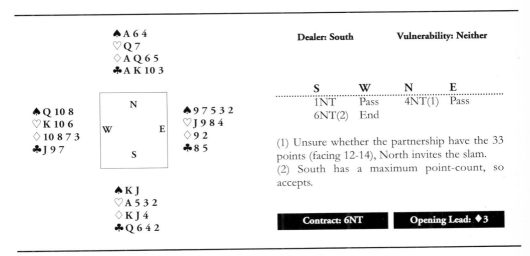

Dealer: South   **Vulnerability: Neither**

S	W	N	E
1NT	Pass	4NT(1)	Pass
6NT(2)	End		

(1) Unsure whether the partnership have the 33 points (facing 12-14), North invites the slam.
(2) South has a maximum point-count, so accepts.

Contract: 6NT   **Opening Lead: ♦3**

This deal sees North invite slam, his partner accept, and West lead the three of diamonds. Declarer counts his top tricks: two spades, one heart, four diamonds and three clubs - total ten. The fourth round of clubs offers an excellent chance of an eleventh trick, but the twelfth will have to come from a successful major-suit finesse (either leading towards dummy's queen of hearts hoping West has the king; or leading to his jack of spades hoping East has the queen).

Because a losing spade finesse would preclude the chance of establishing the queen of hearts (a second trick would have to be lost first), declarer must lead to the queen of hearts first. Declarer made no mistake. He won Trick One with the jack of diamonds, and immediately led a low heart. West played low (the king works no better) so dummy's queen scored.

Declarer now checked his fourth club trick was forthcoming. He cashed dummy's ace of clubs, crossed to the queen (good - both followed), returned to dummy's king (felling West's jack) then cashed the ten. He crossed to the king of diamonds, returned to the ace-queen, and took the ace-king of spades and ace of hearts.

12 tricks. Slam made.

Deal 5

A 2NT response to a 1NT opener shows 11-12 points and is invitational to game, saying "Partner, are you minimum or maximum for your bid?".

A 4NT response to a 1NT or 2NT opener is invitational to slam and asks the same question. Opener passes 4NT with a minimum, and bids 6NT with a maximim. To make this bid over 1NT, responder should have 19-20 points; to make it over 2NT, he should have 11-12 points.

This South opened 2NT with 21 - exactly in the middle of his point range. When his partner invited slam by jumping to 4NT, he was in a quandary. He was neither minimum (20) nor maximum (22). Should he or shouldn't he accept?

The key here is whether he has a good 21 point hand. Aces, kings, queens and jacks are not the be-all and end-all. Tens and nines are important too; as are five-card suits. South accepted the invitation - look at all these positive features in his hand.

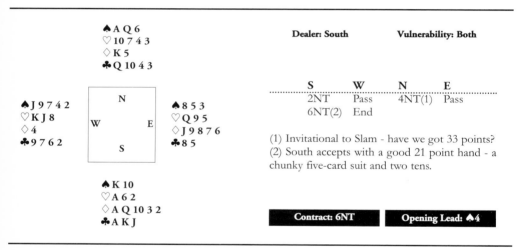

♠ A Q 6
♡ 10 7 4 3
◇ K 5
♣ Q 10 4 3

♠ J 9 7 4 2
♡ K J 8
◇ 4
♣ 9 7 6 2

♠ 8 5 3
♡ Q 9 5
◇ J 9 8 7 6
♣ 8 5

♠ K 10
♡ A 6 2
◇ A Q 10 3 2
♣ A K J

Dealer: South   **Vulnerability: Both**

S	W	N	E
2NT	Pass	4NT(1)	Pass
6NT(2)	End		

(1) Invitational to Slam - have we got 33 points?
(2) South accepts with a good 21 point hand - a chunky five-card suit and two tens.

Contract: 6NT   **Opening Lead: ♠4**

West led the four of spades (a heart lead would have been best, but is impossible to find from such a broken-honour holding). Declarer counted 11 top tricks: three spades, one heart, three diamonds and four clubs.

The five-card diamond suit would have to provide the extra trick, so declarer won the first trick with his ten of spades, led to dummy's king of diamonds and returned a diamond, East following small. He was just about to play his queen when he paused for thought.

All declarer needed was one extra diamond trick. This would be guaranteed if he finessed

his ten (key play). If the ten lost to West's jack, then the suit was splitting no worse than 4-2, and the fifth card would be good after cashing the ace-queen. If the ten won, he was home and dry.

West discarded on the ten, so the finesse had been vital. Declarer cashed the ace-queen of the suit, then the ace-king of clubs. He overtook the jack with the queen and cashed the ten, and finally took the ace-queen of spades, and ace of hearts.
12 tricks. Slam made.

Deal 6

Bidding when a fit is found early is a pleasurable affair. It is purely a question of level.

With shapely fitting hands, high-card points do not tell the full story. Nor does adding an artificial number of points for shortages (although supporting hands can add about three for a singleton and five for a void). The Losing Trick Count is better, but ultimately it boils down to judgement (or "gut feel").

I hope you would bid Six Hearts with North's hand. You have great controls (aces, voids), a wonderful shape (6430), and super trump support. With these essential ingredients, suit Slams can be made with far less than the 33 required for Six Notrump.

Here the partnership actually hold 29 points - not that far short of 33. But take away the queen and jack of hearts, plus the king and jack of diamonds, and the slam would be equally good. Plan the play on a trump lead.

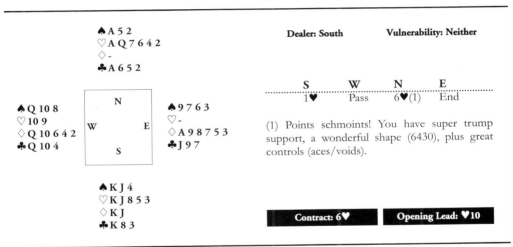

♠ A 5 2
♡ A Q 7 6 4 2
◇ -
♣ A 6 5 2

♠ Q 10 8
♡ 10 9
◇ Q 10 6 4 2
♣ Q 10 4

N
W   E
S

♠ 9 7 6 3
♡ -
◇ A 9 8 7 5 3
♣ J 9 7

♠ K J 4
♡ K J 8 5 3
◇ K J
♣ K 8 3

Dealer: South   **Vulnerability: Neither**

S	W	N	E
1♥	Pass	6♥(1)	End

(1) Points schmoints! You have super trump support, a wonderful shape (6430), plus great controls (aces/voids).

Contract: 6♥   **Opening Lead: ♥10**

Essentially you have two chances: a three-three club split with a spade finesse in reserve. The correct line is as follows: win the trump in hand with the jack, and trump the jack of diamonds; cross to the king of trumps, and trump the king of diamonds. Then cash the ace of clubs and lead a second club. When East plays the nine, play low from hand.

West wins the lead perforce. If he started with just two clubs, he will have to lead a spade (around to the king-jack) or a diamond. Because you trumped your two diamonds earlier, you can discard a spade from one hand, and trump the diamond in the other. Your spade loser has vanished.

If West started with three clubs (as on the actual layout), he can only return a club (leading a spade or a diamond will have the fatal consequences outlined above). Win the king of clubs (East following), cross to the ace of spades, and discard the jack of spades on the established fourth club. Slam made.

Only if West has four clubs is the contract still in doubt. He returns a club to your king, East discarding. You now have to take the spade finesse. Cross to dummy's ace of spades and play a second spade to the jack, keeping your fingers crossed that it is East who holds the queen.

Deal 7

Any Slam venture is bound to fail if the opponents have two aces (assuming no voids). So important are aces in Slam bidding that it was only eight years after the formal beginnings of Contract Bridge (on a cruise ship in 1925) that Easley Blackwood invented by far the famous convention in bridge.

A 4NT bid, when preceded by a suit bid, asks partner how many aces he holds.

The responses are:
5♣: No aces (or all four).
5♦: One ace.
5♥: Two aces
5♠: Three aces.

If the partnership hold all the aces and are interested in a Grand Slam (rare) then a bid of 5NT asks partner how many kings he possesses (the responses are the same as above but a level higher).

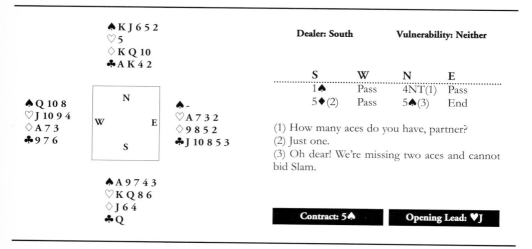

♠ K J 6 5 2
♡ 5
◇ K Q 10
♣ A K 4 2

♠ Q 10 8
♡ J 10 9 4
◇ A 7 3
♣ 9 7 6

♠ -
♡ A 7 3 2
◇ 9 8 5 2
♣ J 10 8 5 3

♠ A 9 7 4 3
♡ K Q 8 6
◇ J 6 4
♣ Q

Dealer: South **Vulnerability: Neither**

S	W	N	E
1♠	Pass	4NT(1)	Pass
5♦(2)	Pass	5♠(3)	End

(1) How many aces do you have, partner?
(2) Just one.
(3) Oh dear! We're missing two aces and cannot bid Slam.

Contract: 5♠   **Opening Lead: ♥J**

Without the use of Blackwood, North would have an insoluble dilemma when he hears his partner open 1♠. If South has the hand he actually holds, with just the one ace, then 5♠ will be the limit. But swap ♥KQ for ♥AJ, and suddenly 6♠ is on the cards.

West led the jack of hearts against 5♠. East won the ace, and returned a diamond to West's ace. West returned a second diamond, taken by dummy's queen, and the only problem for declarer was the queen of trumps.

If the trumps split two-one, as expected, then the queen will fall under the ace-king. But if they split three-zero, he will have to be careful which top honour he cashed first.

Which is the correct one - the ace or the king? Nothing can be done if East holds ♠Q108 - there will be an unavoidable loser as the ♠Q108 lies over the jack. But if West has the ♠Q108, it is imperative that declarer cashes the ace first. If East discards (as on the actual layout), declarer can lead to West's ten and dummy's jack; and follow by cashing dummy's king, felling West's queen.

Contract made.

Deal 8

The Blackwood convention - whereby a bid of 4NT asks partner how many aces they hold - is so alluring that the danger is that it will be overused. It must be borne in mind that Blackwood only addresses one issue - how many aces partner holds; as such it has but one function: avoiding Slams when the partnership are missing two aces.

This deal illustrates that Blackwood only applies when following a suit bid. When the immediate preceding bid is in notrumps, a bid of 4NT is a quantitative bid, asking partner to bid 6NT with a maximum hand for his bidding to date.

Without this arrangement, North has no way to invite Slam. He either has to pot 6NT, or settle for 3NT. The art of good cooperative bidding is to avoid such guesses, but to consult partner.

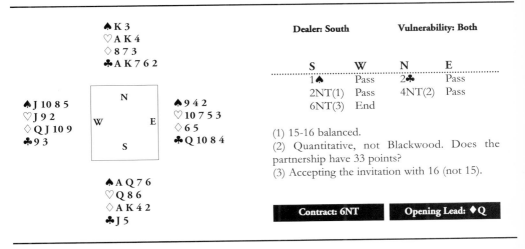

	♠ K 3	
	♡ A K 4	
	◇ 8 7 3	
	♣ A K 7 6 2	

♠ J 10 8 5		♠ 9 4 2
♡ J 9 2	N	♡ 10 7 5 3
◇ Q J 10 9	W E	◇ 6 5
♣ 9 3	S	♣ Q 10 8 4

	♠ A Q 7 6	
	♡ Q 8 6	
	◇ A K 4 2	
	♣ J 5	

Dealer: South   **Vulnerability: Both**

S	W	N	E
1♠	Pass	2♣	Pass
2NT(1)	Pass	4NT(2)	Pass
6NT(3)	End		

(1) 15-16 balanced.
(2) Quantitative, not Blackwood. Does the partnership have 33 points?
(3) Accepting the invitation with 16 (not 15).

Contract: 6NT   **Opening Lead: ◆Q**

Against 6NT, West leads the queen of diamonds - top of an honour sequence - and you as declarer count ten top tricks. The obvious place to look to for the extra two is clubs. How should they be broached?

There are two aspects. One is to try to promote the jack of clubs (a finesse); the other is to try for length winners, keeping tabs of the split.

First the finesse must be tried. That involves leading from the opposite hand to the jack, and hoping that the player playing second (ie East) holds the queen. Win the first trick with the king of diamonds, cross to dummy's king of hearts, then lead the two of clubs towards the jack (key play). With East holding the queen, you are in good shape.

If East plays low on the club, your jack scores; you can follow by crossing to the ace-king of clubs (West discarding), and conceding the fourth round of the suit to East's queen. Win his diamond return with the ace, cross to the ace of hearts, cash the established fifth club and take the last four tricks with the three top spades and queen of hearts. Slam made.

If East plays the queen on the first club, win his diamond return, cash the jack of clubs, cross to the ace of hearts, cash the ace-king and established fifth club, then take the three top spades and two remaining top hearts. Slam made.

Deal 9

Because the responses to the 4NT Blackwood merely indicate how many aces are held, and not which they are, Blackwood should not be bid when holding a void. You will not know whether partner has the ace opposite your void (bad news) or opposite your length (good news).

On this deal, 6♠ would have been doomed if North had held the ace of hearts rather than the ace of diamonds. As it was, the Slam was excellent, though only biddable with some fancy footwork. We will be spending a number of deals on the necessary tools; here is a first look.

South's 4♣ bid is essentially natural, showing slammy values (he has three fewer Losing Tricks than the seven his opening bid implied). It is not an attempt to play in clubs (spades are agreed), but rather for partner to re-evaluate his hand.

With no help in the second suit (honours or shortage), North would sign off in 4♠. However with some help (here the queen), particularly with good trumps, he bids a suit in which he holds the ace (a "cue-bid"). 4♦ (as opposed to 4♥) is just what South wants to hear.

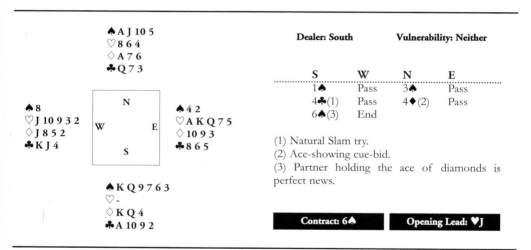

S	W	N	E
1♠	Pass	3♠	Pass
4♣(1)	Pass	4♦(2)	Pass
6♠(3)	End		

Dealer: South   Vulnerability: Neither

(1) Natural Slam try.
(2) Ace-showing cue-bid.
(3) Partner holding the ace of diamonds is perfect news.

Contract: 6♠   **Opening Lead: ♥J**

In 6♠, declarer trumped the jack of hearts lead, and cleverly sought to avoid the possibility of two club losers. Normally the best play missing the king and jack is to run the queen; then, if it loses to the king, to play to the ten. Two tricks are only lost if both the king and jack are "offside". Declarer improved his odds from 75% to 100%.

Declarer crossed to the ten of spades and trumped a second heart. He crossed to the jack of spades and trumped a third heart. He next cashed the king-queen of diamonds, crossed to dummy's ace, and only then passed the queen of clubs. West won the king but had a choice of losing options.

If West led a red suit (declarer had "eliminated" both), then declarer would discard a club from dummy and trump in hand; if West led a club, it would be around to declarer's ace-ten. Slam made.

Deal 10

Last deal we learned not to bid Blackwood with a void, in case partner has the ace in that suit (pretty useless). The way to find out *where* partner has his ace(s) is to initiate an "Ace-showing Cue-bid" sequence.

Here is the procedure:
1. A suit is agreed
2. The first bid of a new suit after suit-agreement is best played as a natural "Trial bid", asking for help in the suit bid.
3. If partner has some help, he can bid a side-suit in which he has an ace (a "Cue-bid").

This deal illustrates the importance of where the ace is held. Swap North's ace of hearts for the ace of diamonds (see last deal), and 6♠ would be an excellent contract.

As it was South was able to find out that North had the wrong red suit ace. His 4♣ Trial Bid excited North (holding the queen of the suit plus good trumps). So he showed his ace. But facing a void, 4♥ was precisely the bid South did not want to hear! So he signed off in 4♠.

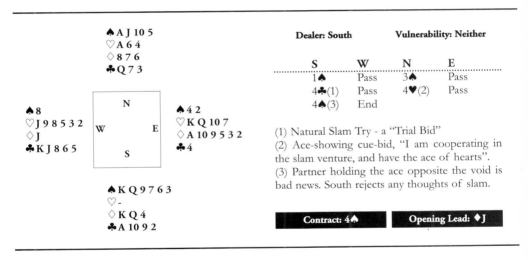

♠ A J 10 5
♡ A 6 4
◇ 8 7 6
♣ Q 7 3

Dealer: South **Vulnerability: Neither**

S	W	N	E
1♠	Pass	3♠	Pass
4♣(1)	Pass	4♥(2)	Pass
4♠(3)	End		

(1) Natural Slam Try - a "Trial Bid"
(2) Ace-showing cue-bid, "I am cooperating in the slam venture, and have the ace of hearts".
(3) Partner holding the ace opposite the void is bad news. South rejects any thoughts of slam.

Contract: 4♠   **Opening Lead: ◆ J**

West's jack of diamonds lead was won by East's ace, and East was able to work out that his partner's led was singleton (West would lead top from a doubleton, and would lead the king from a holding of king-queen-jack).

But East cleverly did not return the suit, preferring to switch to his singleton - the four of clubs (key play). Unaware of the danger lurking, declarer played low from hand. Wrong! West won the king of clubs and returned a club. East trumped and now returned a diamond.

West trumped and returned another club. East trumped and the defence had scored the first five tricks, including scoring all three of their small trumps. Declarer was down two in game when trying for Slam!

It has to be said that declarer should have risen with the ace of clubs at Trick Two. He draws trumps, then leads up to the queen of Clubs, his diamond loser disappearing on the ace of hearts.

Deal 11

We have seen that hands with voids do not lend themselves to Blackwood. Neither do hands with two fast losers in a particular suit. You may have all the aces bar one, but if the opponents can take two quick tricks in that suit, your Slam venture will fail (assuming the opponents lead the suit).

The answer is to use Ace-showing Cue-bidding.

First a trump suit must be clearly agreed. If the next bidder (after suit agreement) could be two-suited (say the bidding has begun 1♠ - 3♠), then the first bid of a new suit is a natural bid, asking for help in the suit bid. However if the next bidder has shown a one-suited hand (this South for example) then the Ace-showing Cue-bids begin immediately.

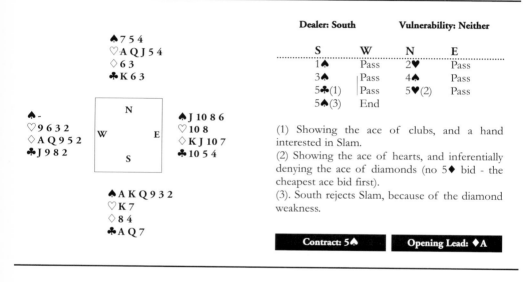

```
                    ♠754
                    ♡AQJ54
                    ◇63
                    ♣K63

    ♠-              ┌─────────┐         ♠J1086
    ♡9632           │    N    │         ♡108
    ◇AQ952      W   │         │   E     ◇KJ107
    ♣J982           │    S    │         ♣1054
                    └─────────┘
                    ♠AKQ932
                    ♡K7
                    ◇84
                    ♣AQ7
```

Dealer: South   Vulnerability: Neither

S	W	N	E
1♠	Pass	2♥	Pass
3♠	Pass	4♠	Pass
5♣(1)	Pass	5♥(2)	Pass
5♠(3)	End		

(1) Showing the ace of clubs, and a hand interested in Slam.
(2) Showing the ace of hearts, and inferentially denying the ace of diamonds (no 5♦ bid - the cheapest ace bid first).
(3). South rejects Slam, because of the diamond weakness.

Contract: 5♠   Opening Lead: ♦A

Settling in 5♠, having found out about the diamond problem, West leads the ace of diamonds (he has been listening too). East encourages with the jack ("throw high means aye"), and West leads a second diamond to East's king. At Trick Three East switches to a club (though if he had led a third diamond - best - declarer would have to trump in hand not dummy).

Declarer won the club switch with the ace and laid down the ace of trumps, expecting to claim his contract if both opponents had followed. When West discarded, he had some work to do. He crossed to dummy's jack of hearts and led a second spade. East inserted the ten and declarer won the queen. He overtook the king of hearts with dummy's ace and led a third spade. He covered East's eight with the nine, and cashed the king of spades felling East's jack. The remaining tricks were his and the five-level contract had squeaked home.

Deal 12

Let us summarise the essential trump slam bidding tools that we have covered to date.

A. *4NT Blackwood:* this asks partner how many aces they possess.

B. *The Trial Bid:* this is the first bid of a new suit after suit agreement (where the bidder can be two-suited). It asks partner to cooperate if he has help in the suit bid.

C. *The Ace-showing Cue-bid:* this occurs only after suit agreement and a Trial bid (if applicable). An Ace-showing Cue-bid is a bid of a new suit,

showing the ace (exceptionally a void) of the suit bid, and a slam-interested hand.

This deal we focus on the Trial Bid. Say the auction has begun 1♥-3♥. If opener has Slam-interest (meaning that he will have about four Losing Tricks), he will often have a two-suited hand. The success or failure of a slam venture will depend on whether responder has fitting honours (or shortage) in that second suit.

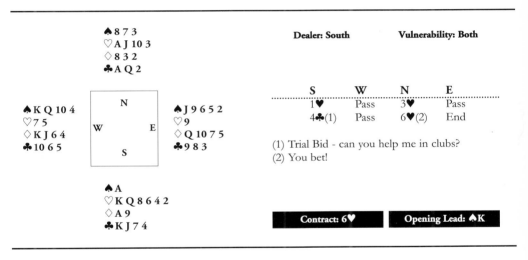

```
            ♠ 8 7 3
            ♡ A J 10 3
            ♢ 8 3 2
            ♣ A Q 2
  ♠ K Q 10 4      N        ♠ J 9 6 5 2
  ♡ 7 5                    ♡ 9
  ♢ K J 6 4   W    E       ♢ Q 10 7 5
  ♣ 10 6 5        S        ♣ 9 8 3
            ♠ A
            ♡ K Q 8 6 4 2
            ♢ A 9
            ♣ K J 7 4
```

Dealer: South   **Vulnerability: Both**

S	W	N	E
1♥	Pass	3♥	Pass
4♣(1)	Pass	6♥(2)	End

(1) Trial Bid - can you help me in clubs?
(2) You bet!

Contract: 6♥   **Opening Lead: ♠K**

Imagine South's dilemma when his partner gives him jump support. With his thoughts turning to slam, he desperately needs to know whether his partner's club holding will prevent losers in the suit. His 4♣ bid does precisely that. It says "I have long (usually four or more cards, occasionally three), weak clubs (usually missing at least two of the four top cards). Can you help?".

If the answer is "No", should, say, North hold three small cards in the suit (can you see how dreadful 6♥ would be if North held three

small clubs?), the reply is a return to game in the trump suit. Otherwise partner does something exciting. His options are to bid 4NT, cue-bid a side-suit ace; or simply, as this North (with his great trumps and clubs), to jump to Slam.

In 6♥, declarer wins the king of spades lead with the ace, draws trumps in two rounds, cashes his clubs, and finally concedes a diamond at the end.

Are you sold on the Trial Bid yet?

Deal 13

Let us review and extend what we know about *The Trial Bid for slam.*

WHEN
It is the first bid of a new suit after trump-agreement. Typical auctions include: 1♠-3♠-4♣; 1♣-1♥-3♥-4♦ (all uncontested).

WHAT IT SHOWS
A long (3+cards), weak (missing two+ high cards) suit in a Slam-interested hand.

WHAT PARTNER DOES
Partner re-evaluates in the light of the new development. With bad hand he returns to the trump suit at the lowest level. With a good hand he gets excited. Before we look at what he actually bids when he's excited, let us focus on how partner decides whether he has a good hand or a bad hand. This is the lesson of the day.

Essentially, partner looks first and foremost at his holding in the Trial bid suit; secondly he looks at his trump quality; thirdly he looks at the rest of his hand - is it minimum or maximum for his bidding to date?

This North had a superb holding in the Trial Bid suit, clubs. Furthermore his trump quality was excellent. So he took control via Blackwood, and bid the Slam when just one ace proved to be missing.

```
              ♠ A K 9 6
              ♡ 3
              ♢ J 7 5 3 2
              ♣ A Q 2
♠ J 8 5 4          N          ♠ -
♡ K Q 9 7                     ♡ 10 8 6 5 4 2
♢ A Q 9     W         E       ♢ K 10 8 4
♣ 9 8                         ♣ 10 5 3
                   S
              ♠ Q 10 7 3 2
              ♡ A J
              ♢ 6
              ♣ K J 7 6 4
```

Dealer: North   **Vulnerability: Both**

S	W	N	E
		1♦	Pass
1♠	Pass	3♠	Pass
4♣(1)	Pass	4NT(2)	Pass
5♦(3)	Pass	6♠	End

(1) Trial Bid - can you help me in clubs?
(2) Yes - so much so that I am taking control. How many aces do you possess?
(3) One.

Contract: 6♠   **Opening Lead: ♥K**

Declarer won West's top-of-an-honour-sequence lead with the ace of hearts and trumped the jack. Expecting an easy ride, he cashed dummy's ace of trumps, but received a rude shock when East discarded.

Undaunted, declarer led a diamond from dummy. West won the nine and tried to cash the ace. Declarer trumped, then played a low trump to dummy's nine. He cashed the king of trumps, led a low club to his jack, then cashed the queen of trumps, drawing West's jack. He then crossed to dummy's ace of clubs (relieved to see both opponents follow), overtook the queen of clubs with his king, then tabled his two remaining clubs. Slam made.

Deal 14

A Trial Bid is the first bid after trump-agreement, asking partner whether they have help in the suit. Though we have focussed so far on Trial Bidding for Slam, the bid is actually far more common in the game zone.

Say the auction begins: 1♥-2♥ (uncontested). Opener must work out whether he has:
(a) no interest in game
(b) a game-invitational hand or
(c) a certain game hand.

The best way to ascertain this is by counting up Losing Tricks (how many of the ace, king and queen in each suit are missing, up to the number of cards held).
(a) No game-interest: a seven (or bad six) loser hand.
(b) Game-invite: a six (or bad five) loser hand.
(c) Game-force: a good five loser hand.

With (a) opener simply passes partner's 2♥. With (c) he simply bids 4♥.
But with (b) he should make a Trial Bid for game. To this end, he bids a long (at least three cards, usually four), weak (missing at least two of the top four cards) suit. This asks partner for help (we will look at his process next deal).

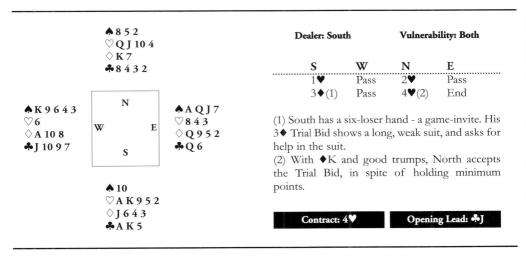

Dealer: South   Vulnerability: Both

S	W	N	E
1♥	Pass	2♥	Pass
3♦(1)	Pass	4♥(2)	End

(1) South has a six-loser hand - a game-invite. His 3♦ Trial Bid shows a long, weak suit, and asks for help in the suit.
(2) With ♦K and good trumps, North accepts the Trial Bid, in spite of holding minimum points.

| Contract: 4♥ | Opening Lead: ♣J |

Reaching 4♥, declarer receives the jack of clubs lead. He wins the king, and immediately broaches his side-suit, diamonds (key play). Apart from trying to promote dummy's king via a finesse, he needs to trump the third and fourth rounds in dummy, so must not draw the opposing trumps (and dummy's trumps) prematurely.

A diamond to dummy's king holds the second trick, and a diamond is conceded to West's ten. Declarer wins his club continuation with the ace, trumps a third diamond (with the ten), leads a low trump to his nine, trumps his fourth diamond with the jack, overtakes the queen of trumps with the king, draws the last missing trump with the ace, and merely concedes one trick in each black suit. Game made.

Deal 15

We are taking a short break from Slams to look at Trial Bidding for game. Understand the principles of the more common Trial Bidding for game, and we can successfully apply them to Slams.

Imagine the auction has begun 1♠-2♠ (uncontested). If opener has a game-invite (typically a six-loser hand) then he can bid a new suit to ask for help in that suit.

Say the auction goes 1♠-2♠-3♣: what should responder do?

The most critical part of his hand is his holding in the Trial Bid (here clubs). He is looking for honours and/or shortage in the suit. The best approach is to count up the number of losing tricks (how many of the ace, king and queen are missing).

(a) Three losers (eg 753, J842). Bad news. Bid 3♠ to sign off.

(b) Two losers (eg 105, Q86, K642). Medium news. Look at the rest of your hand, particularly your trump holding. With good trumps and/or a maximum point-count for your 2♠ bid, jump to 4♠. Otherwise bid 3♠.

(c) One (or no) losers (eg 6, KQ4, A7). Good news. Jump to 4♠.

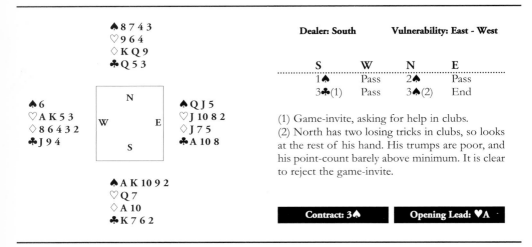

```
                    ♠ 8 7 4 3
                    ♡ 9 6 4
                    ◇ K Q 9
                    ♣ Q 5 3
        ♠ 6              N              ♠ Q J 5
        ♡ A K 5 3                       ♡ J 10 8 2
        ◇ 8 6 4 3 2   W       E         ◇ J 7 5
        ♣ J 9 4                         ♣ A 10 8
                         S
                    ♠ A K 10 9 2
                    ♡ Q 7
                    ◇ A 10
                    ♣ K 7 6 2
```

Dealer: South   **Vulnerability: East - West**

S	W	N	E
1♠	Pass	2♠	Pass
3♣(1)	Pass	3♠(2)	End

(1) Game-invite, asking for help in clubs.
(2) North has two losing tricks in clubs, so looks at the rest of his hand. His trumps are poor, and his point-count barely above minimum. It is clear to reject the game-invite.

| **Contract: 3♠** | | **Opening Lead: ♥A** |

West leads the ace-king of hearts against 3♠, and continues with a third round of the suit. Declarer trumps, and plays out the ace-king of trumps. The hoped-for even trump split does not materialise. Declarer is staring at a trump loser and two almost certain club losers, in addition to the two hearts. Can you see how to avoid the second club loser?

The key is to get the opponent with the ace of clubs to lead the suit. Declarer had to hope that

player was East (for he could be put on play with the third trump). He cashed the ace-king-queen of diamonds, to eliminate a safe exit in that suit, then led a third trump. East won the queen, but was forced to lead a club (to lead a heart would enable declarer to discard a club loser from one hand, and trump in the other). Declarer played low from hand, winning dummy's queen, then led a second club towards his king. All East could score was the ace, and the contract was made.

Deal 16

Regular four-ace Blackwood is a good convention. But not a great one. Look at South's hand on our featured deal.

After opening 1♠, South hears his partner to jump to 4♠ (around 13-15 points or seven Losing Tricks). South is worth a go for Slam, (holding two fewer Losing Tricks than the seven he might have for opening). He bids 4NT (regular Blackwood) and his partner replies 5♦ (one ace). One ace is missing and the question is: should he bid a slam?

Does his partner hold:

(a)		(b)
♠Kxxx	or	♠Jxxx
♥Kxxx		♥KQxx
♦Qx		♦Qx
♣AQx		♣AQx ?

If partner has the Hand (a), a 6♠ contract only requires the three missing trumps to split two-one. A big favourite.

However if partner has the Hand (b), 6♠ has no play at all, losing a trump trick plus the ace of hearts. Playing four-ace Blackwood, South has no way of knowing which hand responder holds.

Because of the limitations of four-ace Blackwood, a Blackwood with "five aces" - the all-important king of trumps counting as an ace - has swept the Bridge world. We will be spending some weeks on this modern variant of Blackwood - known as Roman Key Card Blackwood (RKCB).

As an introduction to the responses (more next deal): with Hand (a) (containing the king of spades) the response is 5♥ (two of the "five aces"). However with Hand (b), his actual one, the response is 5♦ (one or four of the "five aces"). The 5♦ response reveals that two Key Cards are missing (either two aces, or one ace plus the king of trumps), so declarer signs off in 5♠.

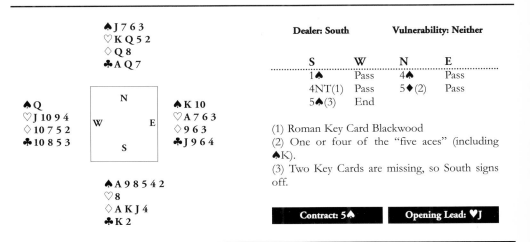

	♠J 7 6 3	
	♡K Q 5 2	
	◇Q 8	
	♣A Q 7	

♠Q	N	♠K 10
♡J 10 9 4		♡A 7 6 3
◇10 7 5 2	W E	◇9 6 3
♣10 8 5 3	S	♣J 9 6 4

	♠A 9 8 5 4 2	
	♡8	
	◇A K J 4	
	♣K 2	

Dealer: South   **Vulnerability: Neither**

S	W	N	E
1♠	Pass	4♠	Pass
4NT(1)	Pass	5♦(2)	Pass
5♠(3)	End		

(1) Roman Key Card Blackwood
(2) One or four of the "five aces" (including ♠K).
(3) Two Key Cards are missing, so South signs off.

| **Contract: 5♠** | **Opening Lead: ♥J** |

West leads the jack of hearts to the queen and ace. Declarer wins the diamond switch with dummy's queen, and leads a trump to the ace.

When both opponents follow to the first trump, all declarer concedes is the second round to East's king. Contract made exactly.

Deal 17

We are learning the modern form of Blackwood, Roman Key Card Blackwood (RKCB). This convention appreciates that the king of trumps is as important as an ace when it comes to bidding slams, and so treats it exactly as though it was an ace.

The responses to the 4NT (RKCB) are:

5♣: *Zero or three of the "five aces".*
5♦: *One or four of the "five aces".*
5♥ & 5♠: *Two of the "five aces".*

(Next deal I'll explain why both 5♥ and 5♠ show two.)

There is some memory work to learn these bids, but you might find the following tip useful: there are three leaves to the club symbol, and four corners to the diamond symbol.

On our featured deal, South is glad to be playing RKCB, rather than the more old-fashioned variety of Blackwood. Playing simple four-ace Blackwood, the bad old days, North would respond 5♥, to show two of the four aces. South would be left guessing whether North's trumps were good enough to make the suit play for no loser.

However playing RKCB, South knows that his partner has either three proper aces, or two aces plus the king of trumps. Either way, he should be in a good position to make all the tricks bar that one missing Key Card.

♠ A K 6 5 2
♡ K 8 6 5
♦ 9 6
♣ A 5

♠ J 9 8 7
♡ -
♦ K Q 5 4 3 2
♣ J 8 3

	N	
W		E
	S	

♠ Q 10 3
♡ Q 10 7
♦ A J 10 7
♣ 10 4 2

♠ 4
♡ A J 9 4 3 2
♦ 8
♣ K Q 9 7 6

Dealer: North   **Vulnerability: Both**

S	W	N	E
		1♠	Pass
2♥	Pass	4♥	Pass
4NT(1)	Pass	5♣(2)	Pass
6♥(3)	End		

(1) Roman Key Card Blackwood.
(2) Zero or three of the "five aces".
(3) North can hardly have no Key Cards for his earlier bidding, so South, relying on three Key Cards opposite, bids a Small Slam. He expects that the one missing Key Card will be his only loser.

Contract: 6♥   **Opening Lead: ♦K**

West led the king of diamonds against 6♥ and, when it won, followed with a second diamond, declarer trumping. At Trick Two, declarer led a trump to dummy's king (key play). It was correct to lead to the king, rather than cash the ace, in order to preserve a possible finessing position (ace-jack).

This precaution proved necessary, as West discarded on the first trump. Declarer was then able to lead a second trump from dummy, to East's ten and his jack. He drew East's queen with his ace, and then turned to clubs. The ace-king-queen of the suit revealed the even split, so declarer could cash his two remaining clubs, and claim his slam.

Deal 18

Playing the excellent modern version of Blackwood, known as Roman Key Card Blackwood, the responses to the Four Notrump bid are as follows (bearing in mind that the king of trumps is the fifth "ace"):

5♣: Zero or three of the "five aces".
5♦: One or four of the "five aces".
5♥: Two of the "five aces".
5♠: Two of the "five aces".

Question: why do both 5♥ and 5♠ show two "aces"?

Answer: Because one response (5♥) denies the queen of trumps; and the other (5♠) shows the queen of trumps.

The importance of the queen of trumps in Slam situations is clearly illustrated by this deal. Make North's queen of trumps into a small trump, and now the slam is hopeless - losing (at least) one trump trick in addition to the ace of clubs.

Without the queen of trumps North would reply 5♥ to the 4NT, and now South could sign off in 5♠. As it was, South was able to bid 6♠.

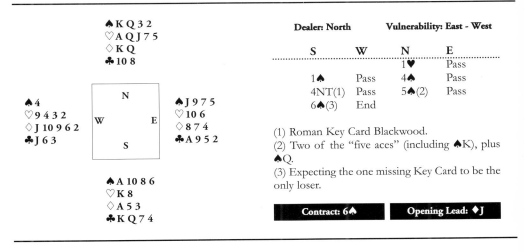

	♠ K Q 3 2
	♡ A Q J 7 5
	◇ K Q
	♣ 10 8

♠ 4		♠ J 9 7 5
♡ 9 4 3 2	N	♡ 10 6
◇ J 10 9 6 2	W E	◇ 8 7 4
♣ J 6 3	S	♣ A 9 5 2

	♠ A 10 8 6
	♡ K 8
	◇ A 5 3
	♣ K Q 7 4

Dealer: North   **Vulnerability: East - West**

S	W	N	E
		1♥	Pass
1♠	Pass	4♠	Pass
4NT(1)	Pass	5♠(2)	Pass
6♠(3)	End		

(1) Roman Key Card Blackwood.
(2) Two of the "five aces" (including ♠K), plus ♠Q.
(3) Expecting the one missing Key Card to be the only loser.

Contract: 6♠   **Opening Lead: ◇J**

West led the jack of diamonds to dummy's queen. Declarer's only concern was the trump split. To cater to East holding ♠J9xx (there was nothing he could do about West holding ♠J9xx), he cashed dummy's king-queen of trumps at the next two tricks, preserving his ace-ten as a finessing position should West discard on the second round.

Declarer's care was rewarded when West did indeed prove to have just one spade. He was able to play a third spade to East's nine and his ten.

Declarer drew East's jack with his ace, then moved to hearts. He cashed the king, and crossed to the ace-queen-jack (discarding two clubs). Leaving the fifth heart (which would squeeze his hand), he cashed the king of diamonds, then led a club towards his king-queen. East played low, so he won the queen, cashed the ace of diamonds, and gave up the last trick to East's ace of clubs. Slam made.

Deal 19

I hope you are enjoying learning Roman Key Card Blackwood, the modern variant of Easley Blackwood's famous convention, which finds out about the king and queen of trumps in addition to the four aces.

Here are the responses to 4NT, with the king of trumps acting as the "fifth ace":

5♣: Zero or three of the "five aces".
5♦: One or four of the "five aces".
5♥: Two of the "five aces", no trump queen.
5♠: Two of the "five aces", plus the trump queen.

Question: Whilst you can show or deny the queen of trumps when you have two of the "five aces", how can you do it when you have a different number (i.e. when the reply to 4NT is 5♣ or 5♦)?

Answer: Your first response does not tell the 4NT bidder whether or not you hold the queen. However if the 4NT bidder wishes to know, he bids the next suit up* (5♦ over a 5♣ response and 5♥ over a 5♦ response). This asks responder to bid Five of the Trump suit without the trump queen, and to jump to Six of the Trump suit with the trump queen.

*This next suit up has to be lower ranking than the trump suit. If it is the trump suit itself, then it does not ask for the queen, rather is a sign-off; if it is higher than the trump queen then the partnership are already committed to a small slam.

Say hearts are trumps. Over a 5♣ response, 5♦ asks for the queen of hearts; responder bids 5♥ without the card, and 6♥ with it. But over a 5♦ response, the 4NT bidder cannot bid the next suit up to ask for the queen. Instead a 5♥ bid says "We do not have enough Key Cards for Slam". Responder must pass.

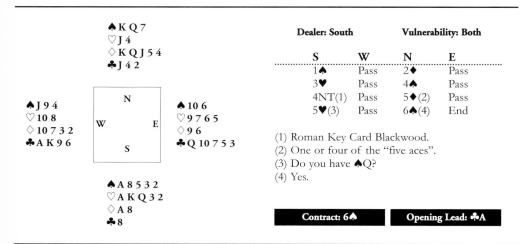

Dealer: South   **Vulnerability: Both**

S	W	N	E
1♠	Pass	2♦	Pass
3♥	Pass	4♠	Pass
4NT(1)	Pass	5♦(2)	Pass
5♥(3)	Pass	6♠(4)	End

(1) Roman Key Card Blackwood.
(2) One or four of the "five aces".
(3) Do you have ♠Q?
(4) Yes.

Contract: 6♠   **Opening Lead: ♣A**

On our featured deal spades are trumps, so South is able to ask for the queen of trumps. In 6♠, West cashes the ace of clubs, then hopefully follows up with the king. Declarer trumps, cashes the king-queen of trumps, and,

pleased to see both opponents follow to reveal the necessary 3-2 split, crosses to the ace. He then runs his plethora of winners in each red suit. Slam made.

Deal 20

We are now in a position to set out in full the responses to Roman Keycard Blackwood: With the king of trumps acting as the "fifth ace", they are as follows:

5♣: Zero or three of the "five aces".
5♦: One or four of the "five aces".

Over both 5♣ and 5♦, the next suit up (not the trump suit) asks partner to bid a Small Slam with the trump queen and to sign off in Five of the Trump suit without it.

5♥: Two of the "five aces", no trump queen.
5♠: Two of the "five aces", plus the trump queen.

The Keycard bidder should be careful that he can cater to any response. As with normal Blackwood, this will be a particular danger when the trump suit is clubs, or, to a lesser extent, diamonds. Even with hearts as trumps, some care is required...

After the bidding began 1♣ - 1♥ - 3♥, South was tempted to bid 4NT (Keycard). Do you see what would have happened? North would reply 5♠ to show his two aces plus ♥Q, and now declarer would know that two key cards were missing, but be unable to play in hearts lower than the six-level. Disaster! Sensibly, however, South resists the temptation.

Dealer: North   **Vulnerability: East - West**

S	W	N	E
		1♣	Pass
1♥	Pass	3♥(1)	Pass
4♦(2)	Pass	4♥(3)	End

North hand: ♠ 8 5 ♥ A Q 10 7 ♦ 5 3 ♣ A K J 10 5

West hand: ♠ J 10 9 4 ♥ 8 5 ♦ A 9 4 2 ♣ Q 9 4

East hand: ♠ A 7 6 2 ♥ 3 ♦ Q J 10 6 ♣ 8 7 3 2

South hand: ♠ K Q 3 ♥ K J 9 6 4 2 ♦ K 8 7 ♣ 6

(1) North has six Losing Tricks (♠AK, ♥K, ♦AK, ♣Q). Adding to South's presumed nine (for a One-over-One response) and subtracting the total from 18 gives three. Hence 3♥.
(2) South cannot use RKCB - a 5♠ reply would leave him high and dry. Instead he makes a Trial Bid for the slam, asking for help in diamonds.
(3) With two losers in diamonds (and spades), North signs off in game.

Contract: 6♠   **Opening Lead: ♦J**

West leads the jack of spades against 4♥, and East wins with the ace. Looking at dummy's weakness, East switches to the queen of diamonds at Trick Two, covered by declarer's king and won by West's ace. West leads back a second diamond to East's ten, and the defence have won the first three tricks.

Declarer smiles at his prudence in the auction, as he wins East's spade switch at Trick Four, draws trumps, and claims the remainder. 10 tricks made - but no more.

Deal 21

Roman Key Card Blackwood features in its responses the king and queen of trumps. So it is essential for the partnership to know what the trump suit is.

Usually it will be clear: e.g. 1♠ - 4♠ - 4NT or 1♠ - 3♠ - 4♣ - 4NT. Both agree spades, the bid

and supported suit. What about 1♠ - 2♦ - 2♥ - 4NT or, for that matter 1♦ - 4NT?

The answer is that in any ambiguity, 4NT agrees the last bid suit (before the 4NT bid). Thus 1♠ - 2♦ - 2♥ - 4NT agrees hearts, and 1♦ - 4NT agrees diamonds.

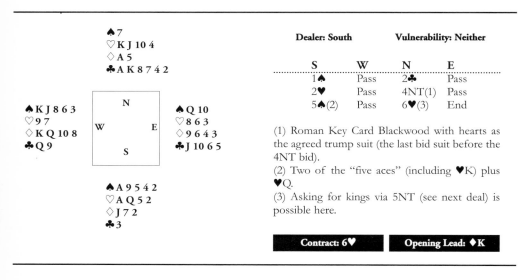

```
              ♠ 7
              ♡ K J 10 4
              ◇ A 5
              ♣ A K 8 7 4 2

  ♠ K J 8 6 3       N        ♠ Q 10
  ♡ 9 7                      ♡ 8 6 3
  ◇ K Q 10 8    W     E      ◇ 9 6 4 3
  ♣ Q 9                      ♣ J 10 6 5
                    S
              ♠ A 9 5 4 2
              ♡ A Q 5 2
              ◇ J 7 2
              ♣ 3
```

Dealer: South   **Vulnerability: Neither**

S	W	N	E
1♠	Pass	2♣	Pass
2♥	Pass	4NT(1)	Pass
5♠(2)	Pass	6♥(3)	End

(1) Roman Key Card Blackwood with hearts as the agreed trump suit (the last bid suit before the 4NT bid).
(2) Two of the "five aces" (including ♥K) plus ♥Q.
(3) Asking for kings via 5NT (see next deal) is possible here.

Contract: 6♥	**Opening Lead: ♦K**

West led the king of diamonds against the 6♥ contract. Declarer won dummy's ace, and correctly began to set up dummy's clubs.

There was a subtle reason why it was better to cash both dummy's top honours, rather than cashing one then trumping a low card. If cashing the ace-king and trumping a third round (with a high trump) revealed that the opposing clubs were splitting three-three, he could now cater to a four-one trump split. He would cash his other top trump in hand and lead over to dummy's king-jack-ten, drawing all four of the hypothetical opposing four-card trump holding, before running dummy's established clubs. If, however, he cashed a top

club and ruffed a low club, he would not know whether the clubs were splitting evenly, and whether he needed to ruff a second low club (in which case he could not cater to four-one trumps).

After cashing ace-king of clubs and trumping a low club with the queen, the four-two club split was revealed (West discarding). Declarer now knew that he needed the trumps to split three-two, so he led to dummy's ten of trumps, trumped a fourth club with the ace of trumps, then led to dummy's king-jack of trumps. He cashed the two established clubs, and just conceded the last trick in diamonds. Slam made.

Deal 22

My advice in general about bidding Grand Slams is simple: *Don't*.

However there will be the odd occasion where a Grand Slam rates to be on, provided partner has all the keycards and the other kings. After discovering that all the keycards (including the king and queen of trumps) are held via Roman Key Card Blackwood, the 4NT bidder has the option of continuing with 5NT to ask about kings. Remember that there are only three kings (the king of trumps is counted as an "ace").

There are two reply-methods to the 5NT bid:

(1) To bid specific kings, cheapest first, provided they are lower ranking than the trump suit; and to bid Six of the agreed trump suit without a king.

(2) To bid 6♣ with none of the three kings; 6♦ with one; 6♥ with two; and 6♠ with all three.

In truth method (1) has a small technical edge - you can discover which king(s) partner holds and not merely how many. But because that edge is so slight, I will be teaching method (2). It is rather easier to learn and to remember - because it is the same as in ordinary four-ace Blackwood.

Dealer: North   **Vulnerability: East - West**

```
              ♠ K 4 2
              ♡ K 6 4
              ◇ A 7 5 3
              ♣ K 8 7

 ♠ 9 8 5            N            ♠ Q J 10 6 3
 ♡ 9 8 3 2     W         E      ♡ 5
 ◇ Q J 10 6                     ◇ 9 4 2
 ♣ 9 4             S            ♣ 10 6 5 3

              ♠ A 7
              ♡ A Q J 10 7
              ◇ K 8
              ♣ A Q J 2
```

S	W	N	E
		1NT	Pass
3♥(1)	Pass	4♥	Pass
4NT(2)	Pass	5♥(3)	Pass
5NT(4)	Pass	6♥(5)	Pass
7♥(6)	End		

(1) Not playing Transfers.
(2) Roman Key Card Blackwood.
(3) Two of the "five aces" including ♥K; no ♥Q.
(4) How many of the other three kings?
(5) Two.
(6) South can count 13 tricks looking at his hand alone, once he knows his partner has ♠K, ♥K, ♦A and ♣K. There are two spade tricks, five trumps, two diamonds and four clubs.

Contract: 7♥   **Opening Lead: ♦Q**

South could count 13 tricks in the auction, given his partner's replies to the 4NT and 5NT bids. So he bid 7♥ - though perhaps he should have bid 7NT in case East unexpectedly trumped West's opening lead. Perhaps he was greedy for his extra 100 for honours in trumps?

Declarer won West's queen of diamonds lead, drew trumps in four rounds, and simply cashed his winners. Grand Slam made.

Deal 23

Last deal we learned that a 5NT bid, when following a 4NT bid and its reply, asks partner about their kings. However whether the 4NT bid was regular Blackwood or Roman Key Card Blackwood (RKCB), the 5NT bid is, in my experience, grossly overused.

5NT should only be bid if all the following criteria apply:
(1) *You are actually interested in a Grand Slam.* Given that the 5NT bid carries you into a Small Slam at the very least, if you are only interested in a Small Slam, then simply bid it!
(2) *The reply to the 4NT indicates that all the key cards are held.* Assuming you are playing RKCB, that means the four aces and the king-queen of trumps.
(3) *There is no reply to the 5NT bid that will leave you*

embarrassed. Say clubs are trumps and you only want to play a Grand Slam if all the kings are held but are missing two. If you bid 5NT and partner replies 6♦ (one king), you cannot revert to 6♣. Oops!

NB: all the above criteria apply both if you are playing RKCB, or just plain old four-ace Blackwood.

For those rare occasions where a 5NT is acceptable, let me remind you of the replies (playing RKCB):

$$6♣ = 0 \text{ kings}$$
$$6♦ = 1 \text{ king}$$
$$6♥ = 2 \text{ kings}$$
$$6♠ = 3 \text{ kings.}$$

NB: that there are only three kings, as the king of trumps is treated as an ace.

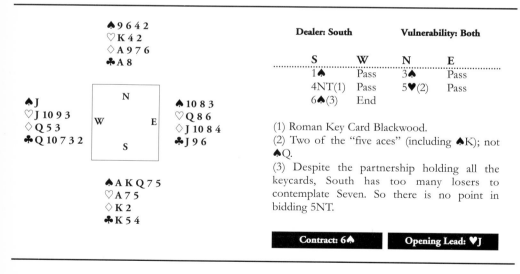

Dealer: South　　　**Vulnerability: Both**

S	W	N	E
1♠	Pass	3♠	Pass
4NT(1)	Pass	5♥(2)	Pass
6♠(3)	End		

(1) Roman Key Card Blackwood.
(2) Two of the "five aces" (including ♠K); not ♠Q.
(3) Despite the partnership holding all the keycards, South has too many losers to contemplate Seven. So there is no point in bidding 5NT.

Contract: 6♠	**Opening Lead: ♥J**

South bid sensibly to 6♠. He won the jack of hearts lead, drew trumps in three rounds, cashed the ace-kings in the minors, trumped the third club in dummy, and merely gave up the third round of hearts. Small Slam made.

At another table (in the Duplicate at my Club), South bid 5NT over 5♥, and then 7♠ over 6♦

(one king). Down one. Yes - he knew all the aces and kings were held. But holding all the aces and kings does not mean all 13 tricks can be made. Recall my general advice about bidding Grand Slams.

Don't!

Deal 24

Roman Key Card Blackwood is an essential tool for bidding Slams. However it should only be used by a player who is ready and strong enough to take control.

Frequently a player has a good hand with some Slam potential - yet does not want to take control (or perhaps is not good enough). Rather, he wants to tell partner something specific about his hand, and see if partner is interested in Slam on that basis.

North's hand, on this deal, is worth 4♠ in reply to partner's 1♠ opener - he has seven Losing Tricks. But playing "Splinter Bids" (our new theme), he is able to bid 4♣. This says, "I have four or more of your trumps, a hand worth (at least) 4♠, and, crucially, a singleton (occasionally a void) in suit I am bidding (clubs). Does that excite you?".

We will be spending several deals on the Splinter Bid, but the general principle is that a double jump in a new suit agrees partner's suit, and shows a good hand with extreme shortage (no more than one card) in the suit bid. It asks partner to re-evaluate his hand in this new light.

On the deal in question, South looks at his club holding, and sees how powerful it has become. His ace will take the first round of the suit, voiding partner; his remaining three cards can be trumped. His 13 point hand has grown in stature to such an extent that he is now able to use Roman Key Card Blackwood, and bid on to a small slam. Note that without the Splinter Bid, North-South would almost certainly bid 1♠ - 4♠ - Pass.

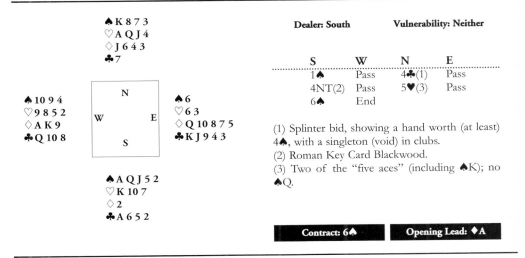

Dealer: South **Vulnerability: Neither**

S	W	N	E
1♠	Pass	4♣(1)	Pass
4NT(2)	Pass	5♥(3)	Pass
6♠	End		

(1) Splinter bid, showing a hand worth (at least) 4♠, with a singleton (void) in clubs.
(2) Roman Key Card Blackwood.
(3) Two of the "five aces" (including ♠K); no ♠Q.

| **Contract: 6♠** | **Opening Lead: ♦A** |

In 6♠, West cashes the ace of diamonds and tries the king. Declarer trumps, and plans to trump two of his club losers in dummy.

Declarer cashes the ace of clubs, trumps a low club, crosses back to the jack of trumps,

trumps a third club with dummy's king, then leads to his ace-queen of trumps. He cashes the king of hearts, and leads to dummy's ace-queen-jack of the suit, discarding his last club on dummy's fourth heart. Slam made.

Deal 25

A "Splinter Bid" is a double jump in a new suit. It shows a hand worth at least game in partner's suit and a singleton (occasionally a void) in the suit bid.

Examples are: 1♠ - 4♣; 1♥ - 3♠; 1♠ - 4♥; 1♥ - 4♦.

Exercise: Partner has opened 1♥. What should you respond with the following hands?

(a)	(b)	(c)	(d)
♠AQ63	♠Q52	♠6	♠KJ742
♥Q642	♥KJ852	♥QJ64	♥J742
♦7	♦A852	♦AJ863	♦QJ7
♣AJ74	♣4	♣KJ5	♣3

(a). 4♦. You are easily worth 4♥ (six Losing Tricks) with a singleton diamond. Perfect.

(b). 4♣. You are worth 4♥ (seven Losing Tricks) with a singleton club.

(c). 3♠. You are worth 4♥ (seven Losing Tricks) with singleton spade.

(d). 3♥. You are not worth 4♥ - with eight Losing Tricks - therefore are not strong enough for a 4♣ Splinter. Instead make a non-forcing 3♥ bid.

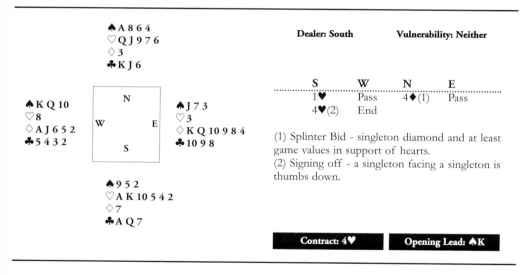

```
              ♠ A 8 6 4
              ♡ Q J 9 7 6
              ♢ 3
              ♣ K J 6

♠ K Q 10            N            ♠ J 7 3
♡ 8                              ♡ 3
♢ A J 6 5 2   W         E        ♢ K Q 10 9 8 4
♣ 5 4 3 2           S            ♣ 10 9 8

              ♠ 9 5 2
              ♡ A K 10 5 4 2
              ♢ 7
              ♣ A Q 7
```

Dealer: South   **Vulnerability: Neither**

S	W	N	E
1♥	Pass	4♦(1)	Pass
4♥(2)	End		

(1) Splinter Bid - singleton diamond and at least game values in support of hearts.
(2) Signing off - a singleton facing a singleton is thumbs down.

Contract: 4♥   **Opening Lead: ♠K**

South heard his partner make a 4♦ Splinter Bid in response to his 1♥ opener. This was a trifle surprising - he also held a singleton diamond. Was that good news or bad news?

Very bad news! A singleton facing a singleton invariably disappoints. In spite of holding a powerful hand, South knew enough to sign off in 4♥ (his most discouraging bid). North passed - after making his descriptive bid, he ceded control of the auction to South.

West led the king of spades, and declarer won, drew trumps, cashed his clubs, but had to concede two spades and a diamond. Contract made exactly.

To illustrate the importance of the location of the singleton, swap North's spades and diamonds around. A 6♥ contract would now be easy, and South would know this, holding three small cards in the splinter suit. The auction would go 1♥ - 3♠ - 4NT - 5♦ - 6♥.

Deal 26

We continue our look at one of the most powerful tools for effective Slam bidding - the Splinter Bid. It is a double jump in a new suit, agreeing partner's suit with at least the values for game and showing a singleton (occasionally a void) in the suit bid.

By saying so much with one bid, the Splinterer puts his partner in a great position to judge whether a Slam is likely. Though the rest of his hand (especially his trumps) will be important, the most critical factor for the partner of the Splinterer will be his holding in the Splinter suit.

Facing a singleton in partner's hand, the king, queen and jack are virtually wasted, whereas the ace is not. Having no honour in the suit, but all the honours outside (facing the Splinterer's length), is even more useful.

Having shortage in partner's Splinter suit means that there will be much work to do in the outside suits - third (even fourth) round losers in those suits may well be a problem.

Good Holding: go for Slam (perhaps via Roman Key Card Blackwood).
Bad Holding: sign off in game in the trump suit.

Exercise: Which of the following are good holdings and which are bad ones?
(a) Axxx, (b) KQx, (c) xxxx, (d) KJ, (e) x.

Answers: (a) and (c) are good holdings facing a Splinter. (b), (d) and (e) are bad.

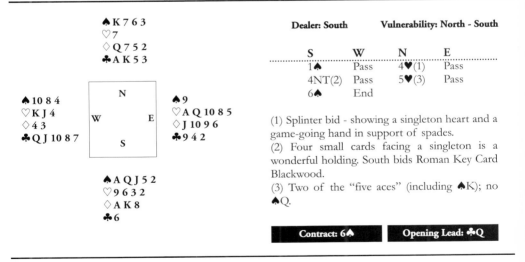

♠ K 7 6 3
♡ 7
◇ Q 7 5 2
♣ A K 5 3

♠ 10 8 4
♡ K J 4
◇ 4 3
♣ Q J 10 8 7

♠ 9
♡ A Q 10 8 5
◇ J 10 9 6
♣ 9 4 2

♠ A Q J 5 2
♡ 9 6 3 2
◇ A K 8
♣ 6

Dealer: South **Vulnerability: North - South**

S	W	N	E
1♠	Pass	4♥(1)	Pass
4NT(2)	Pass	5♥(3)	Pass
6♠	End		

(1) Splinter bid - showing a singleton heart and a game-going hand in support of spades.
(2) Four small cards facing a singleton is a wonderful holding. South bids Roman Key Card Blackwood.
(3) Two of the "five aces" (including ♠K); no ♠Q.

Contract: 6♠   **Opening Lead: ♣Q**

Declaring 6♠ on the queen of clubs lead after a Splinter auction, declarer wins dummy's king, and immediately leads dummy's heart. East wins the ace, and returns the jack of diamonds. Declarer wins the king, ruffs a heart, crosses to the jack of trumps, ruffs a third heart with the king of trumps, then leads to the ace-queen of trumps. He cashes the ace of diamonds, crosses to dummy's queen, cashes the ace of clubs discarding his last heart, and so claims his slam.

Deal 27

I hope you are enjoying learning about the Splinter Bid - one of my absolute favourite conventions. A bid such as 1♠ - 4♣ is useless in a natural sense (with genuine clubs you can just bid 2♣), so why not use it artificially?

A Splinter Bid is a double jump in a new suit. It shows at least a game-going hand with four or more cards in partner's suit, and a singleton (or void) in the suit bid.

The partner of the Splinter bidder is now in the box seat. You should:

(a) *Assess whether you are interested in Slam*, perhaps using the Losing Trick Count (LTC). If the LTC tells you that you are at the Five or Six

Level, then proceed further. If just at the Four-level, merely sign off in game.

Say the auction begins 1♠ - 4♣. If you have seven Losing Tricks, then it is too ambitious to look for Slam. But if you have five or six Losing Tricks, you should proceed to stage (b).

(b) *Look at your holding in the Splinter suit.* Length (three or more cards - the more the better) is good; shortage (up to two cards - one being the worst number) is bad. Holding the ace or no honour is good; holding the king/queen/jack is bad.

(c) *Look at your trumps.* Weak trumps are never an asset, particularly in a Splinter situation where the play often revolves around the handling of the trump suit.

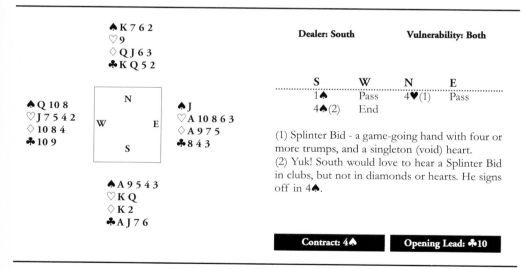

```
              ♠ K 7 6 2
              ♡ 9
              ◇ Q J 6 3
              ♣ K Q 5 2
♠ Q 10 8              ♠ J
♡ J 7 5 4 2          ♡ A 10 8 6 3
◇ 10 8 4             ◇ A 9 7 5
♣ 10 9              ♣ 8 4 3
              ♠ A 9 5 4 3
              ♡ K Q
              ◇ K 2
              ♣ A J 7 6
```

Dealer: South   **Vulnerability: Both**

S	W	N	E
1♠	Pass	4♥(1)	Pass
4♠(2)	End		

(1) Splinter Bid - a game-going hand with four or more trumps, and a singleton (void) heart.
(2) Yuk! South would love to hear a Splinter Bid in clubs, but not in diamonds or hearts. He signs off in 4♠.

Contract: 4♠   **Opening Lead: ♣10**

South held a good looking hand - 17 points and six Losing Tricks. But his partner's 4♥ splinter did nothing to improve it. Quite the reverse - ♥KQ was a terrible waste facing a singleton. Further, his trumps were mediocre. He correctly signed off in 4♠.

West led the ten of clubs, and declarer won and cashed the ace-king of trumps (East discarding). Leaving West's master trump outstanding, he next led the king of diamonds. East won the ace and cashed the ace of hearts, but that was it for the defence. Game made - but no overtrick.

Deal 28

So far we having only considered Splinter Bids as immediate responses to opening bids, agreeing opener's suit and showing a game-going (or better) hand with a singleton (or void) in the bid suit: e.g. 1♠ - 4♣, 1♥ - 3♠, 1♠ - 4♥. But Splinters are so powerful that they should not be restricted to such situations alone. How about opener double-jumping in a new suit after he hears a response from partner?

e.g. (a) 1♥ - 1♠ - 4♣
    (b) 1♠ - 2♦ - 4♥
    (c) 1♣ - 1♥ - 3♠.

(a) 4♣ is a Splinter bid agreeing responder's spades, showing a hand good enough to bid 4♠. In Losing Trick Count terms that means opener has at most five Losing Tricks (a One-over-One responder can be placed with nine). But instead

of merely jumping to 4♠, opener tells partner about his singleton (or void) club en route. If responder has a slammy hand and a club holding that works well facing a singleton, he can go for slam.

(b) 4♥ is a Splinter Bid agreeing diamonds, showing a hand good enough to bid 5♦, with a singleton (or void) heart.

(c) 3♠ is a Splinter Bid agreeing responder's hearts, essentially showing a 4♥ bid with a singleton (or void) spade.

Here are possible hands for opener to fit the three examples:

(a)	(b)	(c)
♠AQ75	♠AK532	♠8
♥AQJ63	♥6	♥AQJ6
♦KJ10	♦AQJ6	♦K62
♣5	♣K72	♣AKJ62

	♠ K Q 10 3	
	♡ A K Q 5 2	
	◇ Q 7 6	
	♣ 3	

♠ 9 8 6 4	N	♠ 7
♡ J 8	W E	♡ 10 9 4 3
◇ J 10 9 4	S	◇ 5 3 2
♣ K J 8 4		♣ A Q 10 5

	♠ A J 5 2	
	♡ 7 6	
	◇ A K 8	
	♣ 9 7 6 2	

Dealer: North   **Vulnerability: Both**

S	W	N	E
		1♥	Pass
1♠	Pass	4♣(1)	Pass
4NT(2)	Pass	5♠(3)	Pass
6♠	End		

(1) Splinter bid agreeing Spades, showing a 4♠ bid with a singleton (void) club.
(2) Four small cards is great news facing a Splinter. South bids Roman Key Card Blackwood.
(3) Two of "five aces" (including ♠K); plus ♠Q.

Contract: 6♠	**Opening Lead: ◆J**

In 6♠ declarer wins West's diamond lead with the king, and plays the ace of trumps and a trump to dummy's queen, East discarding. He cashes the ace-king of hearts, and trumps a low heart with the jack of trumps (key play).

Hearts now set up, declarer leads to dummy's king-ten of trumps, cashes the queen and established fifth heart, then the ace and queen of diamonds. He merely concedes a club at the end. Slam made.

Deal 29

A Splinter Bid is a double jump in a new suit. It shows a singleton (or void) in the suit bid, and a game-going hand with at least four card support for partner's last bid suit. Thus 1♠ - 4♦ shows a hand worth at least 4♠ with a singleton (void) diamond; 1♦ - 1♥ - 3♠ shows a hand worth at least 4♥ with a singleton (void) spade.

Question: does a Splinter always have to be a double-jump, or can it ever be a single jump?

Answer: a Splinter can be a single jump provided it is at the Four-level or higher.

Dealer: North   **Vulnerability: Neither**

S	W	N	E
		1♠	Pass
2♥	Pass	4♦(1)	Pass
4NT(2)	Pass	5♥(3)	Pass
6♥(4)	End		

```
              ♠ A K Q 6 3
              ♡ A J 6 3
              ◇ 7
              ♣ Q 8 6
                    N
 ♠ J 9 5                       ♠ 10 7 4 2
 ♡ Q 10 8                      ♡ -
 ◇ K J 9    W        E         ◇ Q 10 8 5 2
 ♣ A 9 7 4                     ♣ J 10 5 2
                    S
              ♠ 8
              ♡ K 9 7 5 4 2
              ◇ A 6 4 3
              ♣ K 3
```

(1) Despite being just a single jump, this is a Splinter Bid (showing a singleton diamond and a raise to at least 4♥), as it is at the Four-level.
(2) Axxx is a super holding facing a Splinter. South uses Roman Key Card Blackwood.
(3) Two of the "five aces" (including ♥K); no ♥Q.
(4) South knows the partnership are missing one ace and ♥Q. Because he knows only three trumps are missing, he is not worried about ♥Q.

Contract: 6♥   **Opening Lead: ♣A**

North's 4♦ bid was just a single jump. But because it was at the Four-level, it was a Splinter Bid. South, extremely excited by the news that partner had a singleton (void) diamond and a hand worth at least 4♥, bid 4NT (Roman Key Card Blackwood), then advanced to slam.

West, with a good chance of a trump trick, had no hesitation in leading the ace of clubs. He followed with a second round of the suit, and declarer won the king. The contract looked secure, but declarer considered the possibility of a three-nil trump split. If East held ♥Q10x

sitting over the jack, there was nothing he could do. But if West held ♥Q10x, his queen could be finessed provided he retained the finesse position (dummy's ♥AJ).

To this end declarer cashed the king of trumps at Trick Three (key play). East discarded, but, giving himself a mental pat on the back, declarer was now able to lead a second trump to West's ten and dummy's jack, then draw West's queen with dummy's ace. He cashed his winners in the outside suits - he had plenty to spare - and chalked up his slam.

Deal 30

A Splinter Bid is an unusual jump in a new suit, showing a singleton or void in the suit bid, at least four cards in partner's last bid suit, and game-going values or better. By "unusual" I mean that bid has to be a double jump, unless it at the Four-level or above.

The most common Splinter bid is an immediate response to an opening bid, e.g. 1♥ - 4♦ or 1♠ - 4♥. But opener can splinter in support of responder, e.g. 1♦ - 1♥ - 3♠ or 1♠ - 2♥ - 4♦. Taking it one step further, responder can splinter in support of opener's second suit, e.g. 1♠ - 2♦ - 2♥ - 4♣ or 1♣ - 1♦ - 1♥ - 3♠.

Dealer: South   **Vulnerability: Both**

S	W	N	E
1♠	Pass	2♣	Pass
2♥	Pass	4♦(1)	Pass
4NT(2)	Pass	5♠(3)	Pass
6♥(4)	End		

♠ 7 5
♥ A Q 7 5
♦ 3
♣ A J 7 6 3 2

♠ Q 10 6 3
♥ 10 8 4
♦ K Q J 10
♣ 9 5

N
W   E
S

♠ J 9
♥ 9 6
♦ A 8 6 5 4 2
♣ Q 10 8

♠ A K 8 4 2
♥ K J 3 2
♦ 9 7
♣ K 4

(1) Splinter bid, showing a singleton (void) diamond, and a game-going or better hand with four or more hearts.
(2) Delighted at the mesh with his two small diamonds, South uses Roman Key Card Blackwood.
(3) Two of "five aces" (including ♥K); plus ♥Q.
(4) Just what South was hoping to hear. Had he heard 5♥ (two aces but no ♥Q), he would have passed, expecting to lose an ace and ♥Q.

Contract: 6♥   **Opening Lead: ♦K**

Responder splintered in support of opener's second suit, hearts. West led the king of diamonds against the 6♥ contract, and continued with a second diamond. No other defence looked promising, and forcing dummy to use up one of his trumps might prove awkward for declarer.

After trumping in dummy, declarer cashed the ace of trumps, then led a low trump to his jack. Had an opponent discarded, he would have led back to dummy's queen of trumps, crossed to his king of clubs, cashed the king of trumps,

then staked everything on the club finesse, leading to dummy's jack, hoping for West to hold the queen.

But when both opponents followed to the first two trumps, declarer switched to clubs. He crossed to his king, returned to dummy's ace, then trumped a third club with the king of trumps (key play). He next led his last trump to dummy's queen (drawing the last missing trump in the process), cashed the three established clubs, and finally finished up by crossing to his two top spades. Slam made.

Deal 31

The Splinter Bids we have looked at thus far have been in support of a major suit. However let us not overlook the minor suits. Splintering in support of a minor suit is perfectly acceptable, and often an excellent strategy.

Exactly the same principles are used - a double jump in a new suit (single jump OK if at the Four-level) agrees the last bid suit (four or more card support) and shows a singleton or void in the bid suit, in at least a game-going hand.

Dealer: North   **Vulnerability: East - West**

S	W	N	E
		1♥	Pass
2♦	Pass	4♣(1)	Pass
4NT(2)	Pass	5♠(3)	Pass
6♦(4)	End		

♠ K 6 5
♡ A K 6 5 2
♢ A Q 9 5
♣ 8

♠ Q J 10
♡ J 9
♢ 8 7 6 3
♣ K J 9 4

♠ 9 8 7 4 2
♡ 10 8 4 3
♢ -
♣ A Q 10 5

♠ A 3
♡ Q 7
♢ K J 10 4 2
♣ 7 6 3 2

(1) Splinter bid agreeing diamonds, showing a singleton (void) club and a game-going hand.
(2) Hearing the fantastic development (the Splinter bid facing his four small cards), South launches into Roman Key Card Blackwood.
(3) Two of the "five aces" (including ♦K); plus ♦Q.
(4) Delighted at the 5♠ response, South is relieved that the response to 4NT was not 5♥, in which case he would be committed to slam despite missing an ace and also ♦Q. Having said that, bidding a slam depending solely on not losing a trump trick, missing four cards including the queen, is a better than even money gamble.

Contract: 6♦   **Opening Lead: ♠Q**

North splintered in support of his partner's diamonds. His 4♣ bid was a dream for South, whose four small cards in the suit had suddenly become at most one loser. With good cards in the other suits too, South "keycarded" into the slam.

Declarer won West's queen of spades lead with the ace, and led a trump to dummy's ace, observing East discard (a spade). The four-nil trump split was an irritant, but declarer correctly worked out that the contract would still succeed, provided the hearts split no worse than four-two.

At Trick Three declarer led to his queen of hearts, and crossed back to dummy's king. He ruffed a low heart with the ten of trumps (key play), and saw West discard (a club). He crossed to dummy's king of spades and ruffed a low spade with the jack of trumps. He cashed the king of trumps, and led his last (low) trump to dummy's queen-nine (drawing West's trumps). He then cashed the ace of hearts, and followed with the fifth heart. The only trick the defence scored was the very last, a club.

Deal 32

Ideally, a Splinter Bidder should have a small singleton or a void in the suit. Thus 1♠ - 4♣ will usually show a small singleton club, or no clubs at all. Some schools of thought (the "pure" school) veto splintering into a singleton king or ace. They argue, reasonably, that partner will misjudge if he is holding, say, AQJx in the splinter suit. Partner will not remotely expect the suit to play for four winners - which would be the case if the splinterer held a singleton king.

However I love to splinter, and would prefer to make a slightly flawed splinter with a singleton ace or king, than no splinter at all. My advice is not to worry too much about holding a singleton honour, and to splinter in the suit regardless of the chance of partner misjudging.

But note: if you have splintered into a singleton king and partner bids Roman Key Card Blackwood and then asks for kings via 5NT, you must discount your singleton king. Continue to treat it as a low card. (However a singleton ace must be shown as an ace).

Dealer: South   **Vulnerability: North - South**

S	W	N	E
1♥	Pass	4♣(1)	Pass
4NT(2)	Pass	5♦(3)	Pass
5NT(4)	Pass	6♦(5)	Pass
6♥(6)	End		

```
                 ♠ K 6 5 2
                 ♡ K J 9 6
                 ◇ Q 6 5 2
                 ♣ K
   ♠ J 9 8 4           N           ♠ Q 10 3
   ♡ 7                             ♡ 4 2
   ◇ K J 8      W          E       ◇ 10 9 4 3
   ♣ J 9 5 3 2                     ♣ Q 10 8 7
                      S
                 ♠ A 7
                 ♡ A Q 10 8 5 3
                 ◇ A 7
                 ♣ A 6 4
```

(1) Splinter bid, showing a singleton or void club and a hand worth at least 4♥. Yes - ideally the club would not be such a significant honour - but my advice is not to be too much of a purist!
(2) Roman Key Card Blackwood.
(3) One or four of the "five aces".
(4) How many kings do you have?
(5) One. ♥K is an "ace" and, crucially, ♣K must be treated as a small card.
(6) South settles for the small slam, knowing that either ♠K or ♦K is missing.

Contract: 6♥   **Opening Lead: ♠4**

South loved his partner's 4♣ splinter, and immediately had visions of a Grand Slam. But because his partner wisely discounted the king of clubs when asked how many kings he possessed, the partnership was able to stop sensibly in 6♥.

West led a spade, and declarer won in hand, drew trumps in two rounds finishing in hand, then tried leading a sneaky seven of diamonds. Had West ducked, declarer would have won dummy's queen and chalked up an overtrick. But West rose smartly with his king, and declarer settled for Six.

Deal 33

The opposition can take advantage of a Splinter Bid. By doubling, they pave the way for a possible sacrifice.

Sacrificing means bidding a contract in which you expect to fail, hoping to lose fewer points, than defending an opposing contract which you anticipate would make. The vulnerability is a hugely important factor when deciding whether or not to sacrifice. Non-vulnerable against vulnerable is the best time to sacrifice when playing Duplicate Bridge or Chicago (Four Deal) Bridge.

NB: When you are vulnerable, a sacrifice is less worthwhile, and, in such a scenario, the double of a Splinter bid is more of a request for partner to lead the splinter suit, rather than seriously suggesting a sacrifice.

Dealer: South　　　**Vulnerability: North - South**

S	W	N	E
1♠	Pass	4♦(1)	Dble(2)
4NT(3)	Pass	5♥(4)	Pass
6♠	7♦(5)	Dble(6)	End

(1) Splinter bid, showing a singleton (void) diamond, and a hand worth (at least) 4♠.
(2) Suggesting a diamond sacrifice.
(3) South's hand has been upgraded by the splinter - no diamond losers. He bids Roman Key Card Blackwood to find out about ♠K, ♥A and ♣A.
(4) Two of the five aces (including ♠K); no ♠Q.
(5) West knows he won't make 7♦; but, expecting 6♠ to make, he is certain his partnership will lose fewer points playing 7♦ than defending 6♠.
(6) What else can North do? Pass would show a willingness to hear South bid 7♠. It would imply a void diamond (rather than a singleton).

♠ K J 10 8
♡ A Q 10 9 4
◇ 4
♣ J 6 5

♠ 3
♡ 7 6 3
◇ J 10 9 7
♣ K Q 8 4 2

♠ 9 6
♡ 2
◇ K Q 8 6 3 2
♣ A 10 9 7

♠ A Q 7 5 4 2
♡ K J 8 5
◇ A 5
♣ 3

Contract: 7♦ doubled	Opening Lead: ♠J

Left to their own devices, North-South would have made a vulnerable 6♠ slam, scoring 1430 points (at Chicago or Duplicate). They would simply lose one club trick (and only if the defence led the suit).

The 7♦ sacrifice was highly profitable. North led the jack of spades, and South won the ace. Knowing that West held just a singleton spade, South switched to his singleton club (best).

Declarer won and led a trump, but South won with his ace, switched to a low heart to North's nine, and North led a second club for South to trump.

This pretty defence netted North-South 800 points (four down), but that was still 630 fewer points than they would have scored in their 6♠ slam.

Deal 34

It is time to review the key tools in bidding trump suit slams. There are four of them:

(1). *Roman Key Card Blackwood* (RKCB): the modern version of the 4NT ace-asking convention, which includes the king and queen of trumps in the responses.

(2). *The Trial Bid:* the first bid after suit agreement, which asks for help in the bid suit. Thus 1♠-3♠-4♦ says, "If you have a good holding in clubs, we may have a 6♠ slam; if not we should stop safely in 4♠". Note that Trial Bids are equally effective in the game zone (e.g. 1♥-2♥-3♣).

(3). *The Splinter Bid:* an unusual jump in a new suit, which agrees partner's last bid suit. It shows a singleton (void) in the bid suit, and a hand worth at least game.

(4). *The Ace-showing Cue Bid* (ASCB). After either a Trial Bid or a Splinter Bid, the bid of a new suit shows the ace (void) in the bid suit, and slam interest.

Here are some possible scenarios:

Suit agreement (SA) - RKCB...
SA - Trial - RKCB...
SA - Trial - Sign-off.
SA - Trial - ASCB - RKCB...
SA - Trial - ASCB - Sign off.
SA - Splinter - RKCB...
SA - Splinter - Sign-off.
SA - Splinter - ASCB - RKCB...
SA - Splinter - ASCB - Sign off.

NB: there is never a Trial Bid and a Splinter Bid in the same auction.

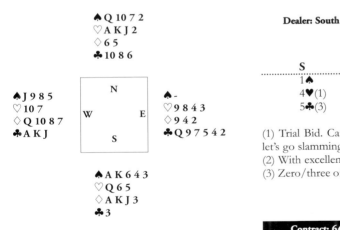

```
              ♠ Q 10 7 2
              ♡ A K J 2
              ◇ 6 5
              ♣ 10 8 6
♠ J 9 8 5              ♠ -
♡ 10 7        N        ♡ 9 8 4 3
◇ Q 10 8 7  W   E      ◇ 9 4 2
♣ A K J       S        ♣ Q 9 7 5 4 2
              ♠ A K 6 4 3
              ♡ Q 6 5
              ◇ A K J 3
              ♣ 3
```

Dealer: South   **Vulnerability: Neither**

S	W	N	E
1♠	Pass	3♠	Pass
4♥(1)	Pass	4NT(2)	Pass
5♣(3)	Pass	6♠	End

(1) Trial Bid. Can you help me in hearts? If so, let's go slamming! If not, please sign off in 4♠.
(2) With excellent hearts, North bids RKCB.
(3) Zero/three of the "five" aces (including ♠K).

Contract: 6♠	**Opening Lead: ♣A**

West led the ace of clubs against 6♠, and continued with the king. Declarer trumped and laid down the ace of trumps. East discarding was a bore but little more.

Declarer crossed to the jack of hearts, and trumped dummy's third club. He cashed the king of trumps, finessed dummy's ten, then drew West's jack of trumps with dummy's queen. He crossed to his queen of hearts, returned to dummy's ace-king, and took the last two tricks with his ace-king of diamonds. Slam made.

Deal 35

We have covered all the important theory. The remaining 15 deals are miscellaneous slammy deals concentrating on our four basic tools: Roman Key Card Blackwood (RKCB), Trial Bids for slam, Splinter Bids, and Ace-showing Cue Bids. They all contain instructive card-play themes.

On this deal, only the Splinter Bid is unrepresented. The key point in the auction is that North would not cue-bid the ace of hearts unless he had something useful in diamonds, partner's Trial Bid. He would sign off in 4♠.

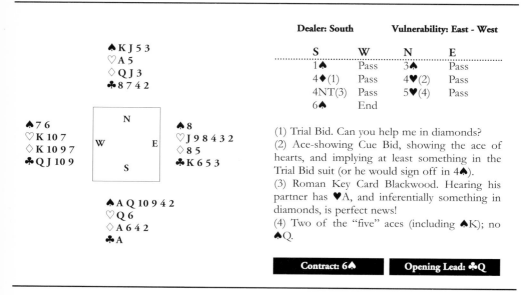

```
                  ♠ K J 5 3
                  ♡ A 5
                  ◇ Q J 3
                  ♣ 8 7 4 2

   ♠ 7 6                          ♠ 8
   ♡ K 10 7            N          ♡ J 9 8 4 3 2
   ◇ K 10 9 7     W       E       ◇ 8 5
   ♣ Q J 10 9                     ♣ K 6 5 3
                      S

                  ♠ A Q 10 9 4 2
                  ♡ Q 6
                  ◇ A 6 4 2
                  ♣ A
```

Dealer: South   **Vulnerability: East - West**

S	W	N	E
1♠	Pass	3♠	Pass
4◇(1)	Pass	4♥(2)	Pass
4NT(3)	Pass	5♥(4)	Pass
6♠	End		

(1) Trial Bid. Can you help me in diamonds?
(2) Ace-showing Cue Bid, showing the ace of hearts, and implying at least something in the Trial Bid suit (or he would sign off in 4♠).
(3) Roman Key Card Blackwood. Hearing his partner has ♥A, and inferentially something in diamonds, is perfect news!
(4) Two of the "five" aces (including ♠K); no ♠Q.

Contract: 6♠	**Opening Lead: ♣Q**

West led the queen of clubs against the 6♠ slam. Declarer won his ace perforce and surveyed the situation. He had a virtually certain diamond loser, so needed to avoid a heart loser. He needed to generate three diamond tricks, which would then enable him to discard a heart from dummy on the fourth round of diamonds. The key was to lead twice towards dummy's queen-jack of diamonds, and NOT to lead an honour from dummy.

Declarer crossed to the king of trumps at Trick Two, then returned to his ace. He then led a low diamond from his hand (key play). West played low, and dummy's jack scored the trick (good - West must be the owner of the king, or East would have beaten dummy's honour).

Declarer trumped a club to return to his hand, then led a second low diamond. West flew in with his king this time, and could do no better than lead a third club. Declarer trumped in hand, crossed to the queen of diamonds, trumped a fourth club, then cashed the ace of diamonds discarding dummy's low heart. Dummy's three remaining cards were the ace of hearts and two trumps. The slam was made.

Note that had the low diamond to dummy's jack lost to the king in East's hand, declarer would have needed a three-three split in the suit in order to have his third diamond trick - and the heart discard from dummy.

Deal 36

On this miscellaneous Slam deal (actually an abortive Slam venture), declarer had to decide which opponent was more likely to have all the three missing trumps. Cover up their hands before reading on.

Naturally declarer hoped that the trump suit would split two-one, in which case the queen would fall under the ace-king. But the decision as to which of his top honours to play first was predicated on which opponent was more likely to hold all three trumps. If West, it would be necessary to play the ace of trumps first; then, if East discarded, he would be able to take a marked finesse against West's queen, leading to dummy's jack and cashing the king. If East, he needed to play dummy's king first, leaving him able to take the marked finesse against East's queen, should West discard.

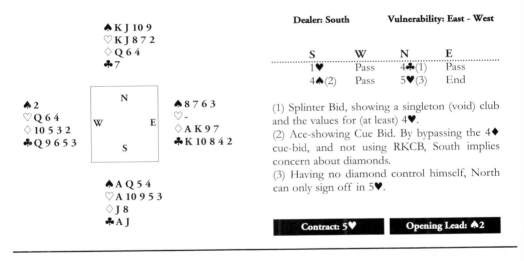

♠ K J 10 9
♡ K J 8 7 2
◇ Q 6 4
♣ 7

♠ 2
♡ Q 6 4
◇ 10 5 3 2
♣ Q 9 6 5 3

♠ 8 7 6 3
♡ -
◇ A K 9 7
♣ K 10 8 4 2

♠ A Q 5 4
♡ A 10 9 5 3
◇ J 8
♣ A J

Dealer: South   Vulnerability: East - West

S	W	N	E
1♥	Pass	4♣(1)	Pass
4♠(2)	Pass	5♥(3)	End

(1) Splinter Bid, showing a singleton (void) club and the values for (at least) 4♥.
(2) Ace-showing Cue Bid. By bypassing the 4◆ cue-bid, and not using RKCB, South implies concern about diamonds.
(3) Having no diamond control himself, North can only sign off in 5♥.

Contract: 5♥   Opening Lead: ♠2

West led the two of spades against the 5♥ contract. Which opponent (if either) do you think is more likely to hold all three missing trumps. Why?

There is something curious. West did not lead a diamond. If the auction is to be believed, it was the lack of a diamond control in either hand that had prevented North-South from bidding a slam. West must have had a good reason to prefer a spade lead to a diamond, and that reason has to be that West's two of spades was singleton. (Perhaps he should have led a diamond anyway).

Assuming that West holds a singleton spade, he is most unlikely to have a void trump; that would give him 12 minor suit cards, and he might have entered the bidding. West is far more likely than his partner to have all three trumps.

At the table declarer reasoned as above and made no mistake. He won the spade lead, and cashed the ace of trumps (key play). East did indeed discard, so declarer took the marked finesse of dummy's jack of trumps, cashed the king (felling West's queen), and merely conceded two diamonds. Contract made.

Deal 37

This deal we see one of the prime advantages of the Ace-Showing Cue-Bid. When a player holds a void, he needs to know which ace(s) his partner holds, not merely how many (as in Roman Key Card Blackwood).

With his five-loser hand, South knew (once his partner jumped to 3♠) that a slam might be on, if his partner held suitable cards. His 4♣ Trial Bid asked for help in the suit, and he eagerly awaited the response. If you swap North's red suits, North would reply 4♦, an Ace-Showing Cue-Bid promising the ace of diamonds (and not a bad club holding - such as three small cards). South would then have been able to pot 6♠.

In fact North cue-bid 4♥, to show his ace of hearts: just what South did <u>not</u> want to hear - he needed North's strength to be outside hearts, where honours would be wasted (facing the void). He signed off in 4♠.

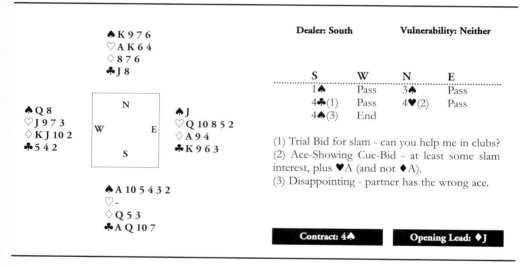

Dealer: South **Vulnerability: Neither**

S	W	N	E
1♠	Pass	3♠	Pass
4♣(1)	Pass	4♥(2)	Pass
4♠(3)	End		

(1) Trial Bid for slam - can you help me in clubs?
(2) Ace-Showing Cue-Bid - at least some slam interest, plus ♥A (and not ♦A).
(3) Disappointing - partner has the wrong ace.

Contract: 4♠   **Opening Lead: ♦J**

The trouble with such accurate scientific bidding is that the opponents are also listening. West suspected that diamonds were North-South's weakness, and began with the jack of the suit. East won the ace, and returned the nine to declarer's queen and West's king. West cashed the ten of diamonds and, seeing no hope of a trick in hearts or clubs (even though his partner held the king of clubs, declarer would finesse him for the card, and so avoid a loser), West tried the effect of leading his fourth diamond.

Good move - dummy discarded a club and East trumped with his jack. Declarer overtrumped with the ace, and had the problem of picking up the queen of trumps.

Declarer used the Principle of Restricted Choice - when an opponent has played a critical card in a suit, his partner is twice as likely to have the adjacent card. Playing West for the queen, declarer led a low spade and finessed dummy's nine (key play). East duly discarded, so he cashed the king of trumps (felling West's queen), crossed to the ace of clubs, trumped a club, and discarded the other clubs on the ace-king of hearts. 10 tricks and game made.

Deal 38

This Slam deal sees North-South cope efficiently with East-West's intervention. Indeed the key bid of their auction is North's Splinter Bid in the opponents' suit.

West led the king of hearts against the slam. When it held the trick, he switched to a low diamond (best). Declarer played low from dummy, and beat East's queen with his king, preserving the ace of diamonds as a late entry to dummy's promising club suit.

If the opposing clubs were splitting three-three, declarer would have an easy ride (with five tricks in the suit). But such a split is against the odds, and declarer sought to find the best route to success on the more likely four-two club split. In that case, declarer would have four club tricks (he would need to trump a round), four trumps and two diamonds. He needed two extra trump tricks - which would come from trumping hearts.

```
              ♠ K Q 7 6
              ♡ 5
              ◇ A 8 4
              ♣ A Q 7 4 3

♠ 10 9 2           N           ♠ 8 4
♡ K Q 2                        ♡ A J 10 9 8
◇ J 9 2      W         E       ◇ Q 10 7 6
♣ J 9 6 2                      ♣ 10 8
                   S
              ♠ A J 5 3
              ♡ 7 6 4 3
              ◇ K 5 3
              ♣ K 5
```

Dealer: North   **Vulnerability: North - South**

S	W	N	E
		1♣	1♥
1♠	2♥	4♥(1)	Pass
4NT(2)	Pass	5♣(3)	Pass
5♦(4)	Pass	6♠	End

(1) Splinter Bid, showing a singleton (void) heart, primary spade support, and at least the values for game.
(2) Excited by the Splinter, South uses Roman Key Card Blackwood.
(3) Zero/three of the "five" aces (including ♠K).
(4) Have you got ♠Q? If so, bid 6♠; if not bid 5♠.

Contract: 6♠   **Opening Lead: ♥K**

At Trick Three declarer trumped a heart in dummy. He then cashed the king of trumps and led a low trump to his jack. If an opponent had shown out on the second round of trumps, revealing a four-one split in the suit, declarer would need a three-three club split. He would cross over to the queen of trumps, return to the king of clubs, cash the ace of trumps discarding dummy's low diamond, then lead to dummy's ace-queen of clubs hoping to catch the four remaining clubs.

In fact both opponents followed to two rounds of trumps, and he was now able to cater to a four-two club split. He ruffed a third round of hearts with the queen of trumps, crossed to the king of clubs, cashed the ace of trumps discarding dummy's low diamond, crossed to the ace-queen of clubs (East discarding on the third round), trumped a fourth club, then, at Trick 12, led to dummy's ace of diamonds.

He took the last trick with the established fifth club. Slam made.

Deal 39

This slam deal features an auction in which responder splinters in support of opener's second suit. Opener is suddenly able to look at his hand in a totally new light, and bids slam via Roman Key Card Blackwood (RKCB).

West kicks off with the king of hearts (with no enthusiasm) against the Six Spade contract, and finds the most testing defence of continuing with a second heart, thus reducing dummy's trump length. After trumping in dummy, declarer surveys his options at this stage. He has three:

(A). To draw the opposing trumps.
(B). To set up his clubs.
(C). To set up dummy's diamonds.

```
              ♠ K Q 7 6
              ♡ 10
              ◇ A J 8 6 4 3
              ♣ 6 4

 ♠ 10 9 2          N          ♠ 8 5
 ♡ K Q 5 2                    ♡ A 9 7 6 4
 ◇ Q 7      W         E       ◇ 10 9 7 6 4
 ♣ Q J 10 2                   ♣ 8 5
                   S
              ♠ A J 4 3
              ♡ J 8 3
              ◇ K
              ♣ A K 9 7 3
```

Dealer: North   **Vulnerability: North - South**

S	W	N	E
1♣	Pass	1◇	Pass
1♠	Pass	4♥(1)	Pass
4NT(2)	Pass	5♠(3)	Pass
6♠	End		

(1). Splinter Bid in support of spades, showing (at least) a game-going hand with primary spade support and a singleton (void) heart.
(2). South's heart problem (three losers in the suit) has evaporated, and his hand is transformed. He asks for keycards.
(3). Two of "five" aces (including ♠K); plus ♠Q.

Contract: 6♠   **Opening Lead: ♥K**

(A) is a non-starter. Drawing three rounds of trumps would leave it too late to try to establish either minor suit. As to (B) versus (C), it is a close decision. Assuming three-two trumps, either line will work if the chosen suit splits three-three. However establishing diamonds will also work on a four-two split if the queen is doubleton. Line (C) is best.

At Trick Three declarer crossed to his king of diamonds. He cashed the ace of spades and crossed to dummy's queen (both opponents following). He then ruffed a low diamond, and, when the queen fell - from West, was home and dry. He crossed to dummy's king of spades (drawing the last trump), and cashed dummy's established diamonds (beginning with the ace-jack). The last two tricks were taken with the ace-king of clubs, and the slam was made.

What a good advertisement the deal is: both for the Splinter Bid (how else would North-South have reached slam?), and for RKCB (letting North divulge the presence of his king and queen of trumps).

Deal 40

This Slam deal features the Trial Bid and the Ace-showing Cue-Bid. On this occasion they were both in the same suit. After North had jumped to 3♥, to show 10-12 points and four-card support, South's thoughts turned to slam. However any slam venture would be bound to fail if North had an unattractive holding (such as three small cards) in South's second suit, diamonds.

How could South ask his partner whether he had useful diamonds? Answer: simply bid the suit - a Trial Bid. A Trial Bid is the first bid in a new suit after suit agreement, asking for help in the suit. If the Trial Bid forces the partnership to at least game (as 4♦ does), then the bid must be a Trial Bid for Slam.

With two honours in both trumps and diamonds, North had too much to sign off in 4♥. But his hand was not powerful enough to take control via Roman Key Card Blackwood (plus he had neither first nor second round control in either black suit). Instead he tried an Ace-showing Cue-Bid of 5♦. This showed Slam interest, but denied a cheaper side-suit ace (i.e. the black ones).

South was happy with the 5♦ cue-bid. Although he knew the partnership was missing the ace of spades, he hoped that the diamond suit would play for no loser (if North held Ax or AQx in the suit for example). His jump to 6♥ was reasonable.

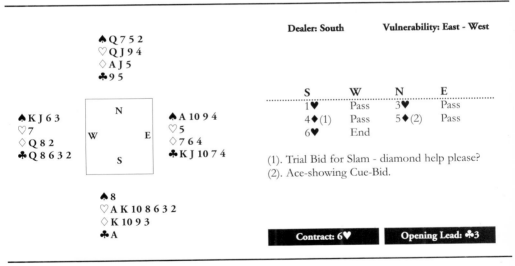

Dealer: South   **Vulnerability: East - West**

♠ Q 7 5 2
♡ Q J 9 4
♢ A J 5
♣ 9 5

♠ K J 6 3
♡ 7
♢ Q 8 2
♣ Q 8 6 3 2

♠ A 10 9 4
♡ 5
♢ 7 6 4
♣ K J 10 7 4

♠ 8
♡ A K 10 8 6 3 2
♢ K 10 9 3
♣ A

S	W	N	E
1♥	Pass	3♥	Pass
4♦(1)	Pass	5♦(2)	Pass
6♥	End		

(1). Trial Bid for Slam - diamond help please?
(2). Ace-showing Cue-Bid.

Contract: 6♥   **Opening Lead: ♣3**

West led the three of clubs, and dummy revealed a gap in diamonds. Declarer had a two-way finesse position in the suit. Who should play for the missing queen? At the table he tried a little psychology.

Declarer won the ace of clubs, cashed the ace of trumps, crossed to dummy's jack, then advanced the jack of diamonds (key play). Because East might cover (or at least flinch) if

holding the queen, declarer drew the correct inference when East followed low in bored fashion. He deduced that West was more likely to have the missing queen.

Declarer rose with his king of diamonds, and then led the ten. West played low, and dummy played low. Bingo! The ten won, so declarer was able to cross to dummy's ace, and claim his slam, losing just one spade trick.

Deal 41

A Trial Bid is the first new suit bid after suit agreement, asking for help in the suit bid. Most of the Trial Bids we have looked at have been made by opener, after his opening bid has been supported. This Slam deal features a Trial Bid by responder.

After his 1♥ response had received jump support, South was in the Slam zone. To test the degree of mesh, he sensibly bid 4♦. After all, if North held three small cards in diamonds, 6♥ would be horrible. In fact North had a brilliant diamond holding, so took charge via Roman Key Card Blackwood.

Dealer: North   **Vulnerability: North - South**

S	W	N	E
		1♣	Pass
1♥(1)	Pass	3♥	Pass
4♦(2)	Pass	4NT(3)	Pass
5♦(4)	Pass	6♥(5)	End

(1) Correctly responding in the higher ranking of two five-card suits ("high-fives").
(2) Trial Bid for Slam. Although his point-count is low, he can envisage a Slam if partner has the right (i.e. red-suit) honours. His 4♦ bid says, "Can you help me in diamonds?"
(3) With fantastic help in diamonds, good trumps, and a side-ace, North launches into Roman Key Card Blackwood.
(4) One or four of the "five" aces (including ♥K).
(5). With no room to ask for ♥Q, North gambles 6♥, expecting partner to have the card to justify his slam try.

```
              ♠ A 4
              ♡ A J 10 5
              ◇ A Q
              ♣ Q 10 9 4 2
♠ K Q 9 5        N        ♠ J 8 7 3 2
♡ 9 3 2      W     E      ♡ 6
◇ 6 4                     ◇ 10 9 8 5
♣ K J 8 7        S        ♣ A 6 3
              ♠ 10 6
              ♡ K Q 8 7 4
              ◇ K J 7 3 2
              ♣ 5
```

Contract: 6♥	Opening Lead: ♠K

West led the king of spades, and declarer surveyed his prospects. He mentally assumed hearts would be three-one and diamonds four-two (the most likely splits - an even number of missing cards does not rate to split evenly). If he drew trumps in three rounds, he would have no way of reaching his hand after cashing the ace-queen of diamonds (unable to spare a fourth round of trumps). He would have to overtake the queen of diamonds after cashing the ace, relying on a three-three split in the suit.

Declarer spotted a better way. He won dummy's ace of spades, cashed the ace-jack of trumps, but left the last trump outstanding. Instead he cashed the ace-queen of diamonds first (key play), and only then led a third trump to his hand. He cashed the king-jack-seven of diamonds and, on one of these, discarded dummy's spade loser. He trumped his spade loser in dummy, and merely conceded one club trick. Slam made.

Deal 42

Holding three small cards in a suit in which partner has advertised length is very dangerous. Holding the king and queen in a suit in which partner has advertised shortage is rather a waste.

On that basis, South might (should?) have shut up shop on this Slam deal. But it's hard to be too negative, when you hold 16 high-card points and you could have held nine. South made one encouraging squeak, and soon found himself declaring a near-hopeless Slam. Could he bring it home?

Dealer: North　　　　**Vulnerability: Both**

S	W	N	E
		1♦	Pass
2♣	Pass	4♥(1)	Pass
4♠(2)	Pass	4NT(3)	Pass
5♠(4)	Pass	6♣	End

♠ K Q 7
♡ 10
♢ A 9 8 7 6
♣ A K 5 3

♠ J 10 9 4 2
♡ J 7 5
♢ K 4
♣ 10 8 2

N
W　E
S

♠ 8 6
♡ 9 8 6 4 3 2
♢ Q J 10
♣ 9 7

♠ A 5 3
♡ A K Q
♢ 5 3 2
♣ Q J 6 4

(1). Splinter Bid, showing primary club support and a singleton (void) heart.
(2). Ace-showing Cue-bid. In spite of holding so many points, South's encouraging noise is (very) marginal. Three small diamonds facing partner's first suit is poor news. How he wished his ♥KQ were ♦KQ!
(3). Encouraged by hearing of ♠A and Slam interest opposite, North bids "Keycard".
(4). Two of "five" aces (including ♣K); plus ♣Q.

Contract: 6♣　　　　**Opening Lead: ♠J**

West led the jack of spades, and declarer viewed dummy. He was staring at two seemingly certain losers in diamonds. Trying to appear confident, he won the spade lead, drew the trumps in three rounds, cashed the three top hearts (discarding diamonds from dummy), and then followed with the two remaining top spades, finishing in his hand.

Declarer reached a four-card ending in which dummy held ♦Axx and a trump, and he held ♦xxx and a trump. He led a low diamond towards dummy, West played low, and he called for dummy's ace (East following with the ten).

He next led a low diamond from dummy, and West won his now bare king.

With West holding only two spades to lead at Trick 12, declarer was able to trump in one hand, and discard his remaining diamond loser from the other. Slam made.

West suddenly realised with horror that he could have defeated the Slam - can you see how? He should have played his king of diamonds on the first round of the suit, to avoid being endplayed with the card. East would have defeated the Slam with his queen-jack of the suit.

Deal 43

This South felt he had just enough to make a Trial Bid for Slam after his partner's jump to 3♥. He chose 3♠ rather than 4♦ - despite needing help in both suits - because it was cheaper, and so gave his partner more room.

I think it was an over-optimistic Slam try by South. It could have backfired by encouraging partner to bid a failing Slam. In fact it backfired in another way...for the opponents were listening carefully to the auction, and found a killing defence.

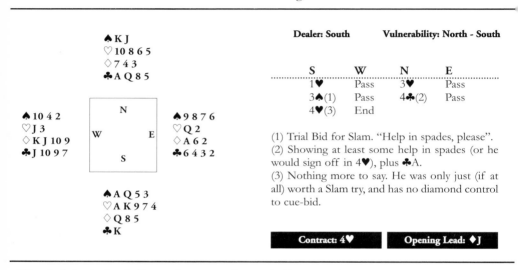

Dealer: South   **Vulnerability: North - South**

S	W	N	E
1♥	Pass	3♥	Pass
3♠(1)	Pass	4♣(2)	Pass
4♥(3)	End		

(1) Trial Bid for Slam. "Help in spades, please".
(2) Showing at least some help in spades (or he would sign off in 4♥), plus ♣A.
(3) Nothing more to say. He was only just (if at all) worth a Slam try, and has no diamond control to cue-bid.

Contract: 4♥   **Opening Lead: ♦J**

West led the jack of diamonds - top of an internal sequence - against the 4♥ contract. Though risky to lead from such a holding, West knew that the opponents were near to slam - both had made slam tries - and that an attacking defence would be necessary to defeat the contract. How true!

East won his ace of diamonds and returned the six of diamonds. Declarer tried the queen from hand, but West won his king, cashed the ten, and then needed just one more trick to defeat the game.

Calculating that declarer had to have good enough black holdings (for his Slam try) to prevent the defence from having a winner in either suit, West realised that the fourth defensive trick could only come from trumps. With this in mind, he led his fourth diamond (key play), even though he knew no other player

held any cards in the suit. Can you see what happened?

Dummy discarded, East ruffed the diamond with the queen of trumps, and declarer was forced to overruff with the king. West could now not be prevented from scoring his jack of trumps. Declarer cashed the ace and conceded the second round of trumps to that card. A perfect Trump Promotion - in the normal course of events the defence's trumps would fall under the ace-king.

South was left to rue the informative auction - never forget that there is a downside to scientific investigation when playing against astute opponents. West's natural lead against an unhelpful auction (such as 1♥ - 3♥ - 4♥) would be the jack of clubs. The 4♥ contract would now romp home.

Deal 44

On this deal North makes a Splinter Bid - showing a singleton (void) in the suit bid, primary trump support and at least a game going hand. Surprisingly, South finds himself staring at a singleton in the same suit.

Yuk! Singleton opposite singleton means that the hands are bound to mesh poorly - one of the singletons being completely wasted. South hurriedly signs off in game. In fact he should not even make 4♠, but, after starting on the right foot, the defence lose their way...

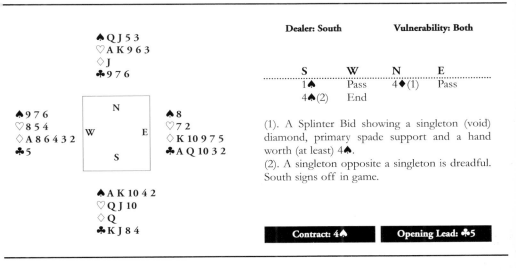

```
            ♠ Q J 5 3
            ♡ A K 9 6 3
            ◇ J
            ♣ 9 7 6
  ♠ 9 7 6        N        ♠ 8
  ♡ 8 5 4                 ♡ 7 2
  ◇ A 8 6 4 3 2  W   E    ◇ K 10 9 7 5
  ♣ 5                     ♣ A Q 10 3 2
                 S
            ♠ A K 10 4 2
            ♡ Q J 10
            ◇ Q
            ♣ K J 8 4
```

Dealer: South   **Vulnerability: Both**

S	W	N	E
1♠	Pass	4◇(1)	Pass
4♠(2)	End		

(1). A Splinter Bid showing a singleton (void) diamond, primary spade support and a hand worth (at least) 4♠.
(2). A singleton opposite a singleton is dreadful. South signs off in game.

Contract: 4♠   **Opening Lead: ♣5**

West naturally began with with his singleton five of clubs. East won the ace, and returned the two of clubs. Not suspecting that the lead was a singleton, declarer rose with the king, trumped by West. Looking at dummy's singleton diamond, West cashed his ace of diamonds, and then switched to a heart. Declarer won in hand with the ten, drew trumps in two rounds, and then cashed the four remaining hearts, discarding his two remaining clubs. Contract made. Where did the defence go astray?

Consider West's predicament after trumping the second club. With the threat of dummy's hearts looming, his main chance of defeating the contract was to put his partner on lead to play a third club (which West could trump again, unless his partner happened to hold the master queen of clubs). He should have hoped that his partner held the king of diamonds, and led a low diamond at Trick Three (key play) instead of the ace. Indeed if East-West were using the suit-preference signal (recommended in trumping situations), then East's return of a low club at Trick Two indicated the desire for West to return the lower ranking of the remaining suits (i.e. diamonds).

East would duly have won the diamond return with his king, and cashed the queen of clubs. Down one. Had declarer inserted the jack of clubs on the second trick, he would have fared no better. East would have led a third club, and West would have trumped declarer's king. Again - down one.

Deal 45

South's first reaction, on receiving jump support for his spades, was to use Roman Key Card Blackwood (RKCB). After all - aces were his main concern. But then his attention turned to his weak diamond holding. If his partner was also poor in that department (say two or three small cards), then any slam venture would be doomed.

Enter the Trial Bid for Slam, South's 4♦ asking for help in the suit. Holding just one Losing Trick in diamonds, plus aces in all three outside suits, it was North who was now able to use RKCB.

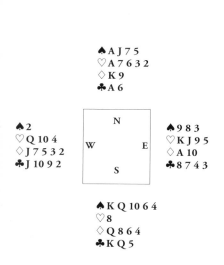

♠ A J 7 5
♡ A 7 6 3 2
♢ K 9
♣ A 6

♠ 2
♡ Q 10 4
♢ J 7 5 3 2
♣ J 10 9 2

♠ 9 8 3
♡ K J 9 5
♢ A 10
♣ 8 7 4 3

♠ K Q 10 6 4
♡ 8
♢ Q 8 6 4
♣ K Q 5

Dealer: North **Vulnerability: Neither**

S	W	N	E
		1♥	Pass
1♠	Pass	3♠	Pass
4♦(1)	Pass	4NT(2)	Pass
5♦(3)	Pass	5♥(4)	Pass
6♠(5)	End		

(1) The first bid after suit agreement is a Trial Bid - asking for help in the bid suit. Because the partnership is necessarily forced to game, this must be a Trial Bid for Slam.
(2) With great diamonds and outside controls, South takes control via RKCB.
(3) One/four of the "five" aces (including ♠K).
(4) Do you have ♠Q?
(5) Yes. Without ♠Q, South would sign off in 5♠. Note that South has no Grand Slam interest so does not bother to show ♣K

Contract: 6♠   **Opening Lead: ♣J**

West led the jack of clubs against 6♠. Declarer viewed dummy, and paused for thought. The most likely trump split missing four cards is three-one; to draw the opposing trumps would probably require three rounds, leaving just one trump in dummy to trump two diamonds. No good. He came to the correct conclusion: drawing trumps had to be delayed.

Declarer won the club lead with dummy's ace, and immediately led the king of diamonds. East won his ace, and led a second club. Declarer won his queen, and cashed the king of trumps

(he could afford one round). Both opponents followed, so he cashed the queen of diamonds (noting East's ten), then trumped a third diamond with dummy's jack of spades (when East discarded, he was pleased he had remembered to trump high). He led the seven of trumps to his ten, and trumped his last diamond with the ace of trumps. He cashed the ace of hearts, trumped a heart, drew East's last trump, then cashed the king of clubs and last trump.

12 tricks and Slam made.

Deal 46

As soon as his partner opened 1♠, this North needed only to find out about key cards. Taking the slight risk of the third round of clubs, the three cards of interest were the king of spades, and the two red aces: perfect for Roman Key Card Blackwood. There was no need for any of our other favourite tools - the Splinter Bid, the Trial Bid, and the Ace-showing Cue-bid.

South's response indicated that zero or three of the "five aces" were held. If both these possibilities are plausible, the 4NT bidder has to assume the lower number and bid accordingly. If the higher number is in fact held, his partner must bid on over the sign-off. As happened on this occasion.

```
                ♠ A 8 7 5 4 3
                ♡ 6
                ◇ 6
                ♣ A K J 8 4
 ♠ -                            ♠ Q 10 6
 ♡ K Q 8 4        N             ♡ 10 9 7 3 2
 ◇ 10 9 7 5 3 2  W   E          ◇ J 8 4
 ♣ 10 3 2          S            ♣ Q 6
                ♠ K J 9 2
                ♡ A J 5
                ◇ A K Q
                ♣ 9 7 5
```

Dealer: South   **Vulnerability: Both**

S	W	N	E
1♠	Pass	4NT(1)	Pass
5♣(2)	Pass	5♠(3)	Pass
6♠(4)	Pass	7♠(5)	End

(1) Takes control: Roman Key Card Blackwood.
(2) Zero or three of "five aces" (including ♠K).
(3) Assuming zero, North signs off.
(4) With three, South bids on to 6♠. It is inconceivable that three "aces" are insufficient for Slam.
(5) Knowing of all three "aces" opposite, North takes a chance on ♠Q (he knows there are at most three missing trumps), and ♣Q.

Contract: 7♠	**Opening Lead: ♥K**

Declaring 7♠, South won West's ♥K lead with ♥A, and crossed to ♠A (key play), preserving his finesse position. His care was rewarded when West discarded. He was thus able to take the marked trump finesse, playing low from dummy to East's ♠10 and his ♠J. He cashed ♠K, felling East's ♠Q, and had one more hurdle to overcome - the third round of clubs.

The odds missing the queen and four low cards were to finesse dummy's ♣J. But declarer arrived at an ingenious end-position. He cashed the ♠9, trumped ♥5 in dummy, cashed ♣A, led dummy's last trump (discarding ♣7 from hand), then crossed to his ◆AKQ. His last two cards in hand were ♥J and ♣9; dummy's were ♣KJ. He led ♣9 and West followed with ♣10. Should he finesse ♣J or play ♣K?

Declarer recalled that West's opening lead was ♥K - indicating ♥Q. West's last card had to be ♥Q, and therefore there was no point in finessing ♣J. Instead declarer rose with ♣K. He was delighted to see ♣Q fall from East. The last trick was taken with dummy's ♣J, and the Grand Slam was made.

A perfect "Show-up Squeeze".

Deal 47

A Splinter Bid is an unnecessary jump in a new suit, agreeing partner's last bid suit, and showing at least game values. Normally "unnecessary" means a double jump (missing out two lower bids of the suit) - such as 1♥ - 3♠ or 1♣ - 1♦ - 3♥. But a single jump is sufficient when the bid is at the Four-level (or above) - such as 1♠ - 2♥ - 4♣ or 1♠ - 2♠ - 4♦.

Thus North's 4♠ bid was a Splinter Bid (agreeing his partner's diamonds). It was the key bid that enabled South to ask for key cards and bid the Grand Slam.

Dealer: South **Vulnerability: East - West**

```
                    ♠ 10
                    ♡ A Q 10 6 5
                    ◇ J 7 6 5
                    ♣ A 8 5

♠ Q 9 5 3 2      N            ♠ K J 7 6
♡ 8 7 2                        ♡ K J 9 3
◇ -          W       E         ◇ Q 8 3
♣ J 10 9 6 4                   ♣ 3 2
                    S

                    ♠ A 8 4
                    ♡ 4
                    ◇ A K 10 9 4 2
                    ♣ K Q 7
```

S	W	N	E
1◇	Pass	1♥	Pass
3◇	Pass	4♠(1)	Pass
4NT(2)	Pass	5♠(3)	Pass
7◇(4)	End		

(1) Splinter Bid, showing a singleton (void) spade, primary diamond support, and a Slam-interested hand.
(2) The Splinter Bid opposite is fabulous news. Time for Roman Key Card Blackwood.
(3) North pretends he has ◆Q. He knows his side has ten trumps, making it unlikely ◆Q will score.
(4) South has no obvious losers.

Contract: 7◆ **Opening Lead: ♣J**

Declaring the excellent 7◆ contract, South received the jack of clubs opening lead from West. He won his queen, and cashed the ace of trumps. There was bad news and good news awaiting.

The bad news was that one opponent discarded - to reveal a three-nil trump split. The good news was that it was West who discarded, leaving East's queen easily finessable. Had East discarded, declarer would have had an inescapable trump loser and his Grand Slam would have been doomed.

Declarer could not afford to draw three rounds of trumps immediately - to do so would only leave one trump in dummy, and he had two losing spades to trump. So declarer cashed the ace of spades, trumped a spade, took the marked finesse of his ten of trumps, trumped his last spade with dummy's last trump (the jack), cashed the ace of hearts, trumped a heart, cashed his king of trumps (felling East's queen), and claimed the last four tricks. They could easily be taken with his two remaining trumps and the ace-king of clubs.
Grand Slam made.

Deal 48

The most common Splinter Bid is a first response to an opening bid; such as 1♥ - 3♠ or 1♠ - 4♦. The bid shows a singleton (void) in the suit bid, and at least the values for game in support of opener's suit.

However once the principle is mastered - that they are unnecessary jumps in new suits - the Splinter Bid can pop up in all sorts of situations. Take this Slam deal.

Dealer: North **Vulnerability: Both**

S	W	N	E
		1♠	Pass
2♥(1)	Pass	2♠	Pass
3♣	Pass	4♦(2)	Pass
4NT(3)	Pass	5♥(4)	Pass
6♣	End		

♠ A K 7 5 4 2
♡ 6 5
♦ 8
♣ K J 6 5

♠ 6 3
♡ Q 2
♦ K 9 7 4 3 2
♣ 9 4 3

N
W E
S

♠ Q J 10 8
♡ J 10 9 4
♦ A Q J 10
♣ 8

♠ 9
♡ A K 8 7 3
♦ 6 5
♣ A Q 10 7 2

(1) Correctly bidding the higher ranking of two five-card suits (he would bid the cheaper of four-card suits).

(2) The Splinter Bid. Agreeing the last bid suit, clubs, and showing a singleton (void) diamond.

(3) After hearing partner bid and rebid spades at the lowest level, South was not thinking of Slam. However the Splinter radically improved his hand, and he chances Roman Key Card Blackwood. I say "chances", because an (unlikely) 5♦ response would leave him (very) awkwardly placed.

(4) Two of the "five"aces (including ♣K); no ♣Q.

Contract: 6♣   **Opening Lead: ♦4**

Declaring 6♣, South received a diamond opening lead (I'm sure West wasn't overjoyed to lead the Splinter suit, but his alternatives were at least as unattractive). East won the ace, and continued with the queen of diamonds (best), forcing dummy to trump.

Declarer sought to establish dummy's spades - and the sooner the better. It was a line that would work, unless spades were five-one or trumps four-nil. He cashed the ace of spades, and trumped a low spade (with the ten), both opponents following. He cashed the ace of

clubs, and led to dummy's jack (East discarding a diamond). He ruffed another low spade with the queen of trumps (West discarding a diamond), then led his final trump to dummy's king, drawing West's last trump in the process.

Dummy's spades were established, and the opposing trumps had been drawn. All that remained was to cash the king of spades, felling East's queen, and continue by leading the two established length winners in the suit. The ace-king of hearts brought his total to 12. Slam made.

Deal 49

It is rare to bid and make a Slam after the opponents have opened the bidding and responded. Rare - but not impossible.

On this deal, North-South brushed aside East-West's spade bidding, even splintering in their suit, to reach the excellent Six Club contract.

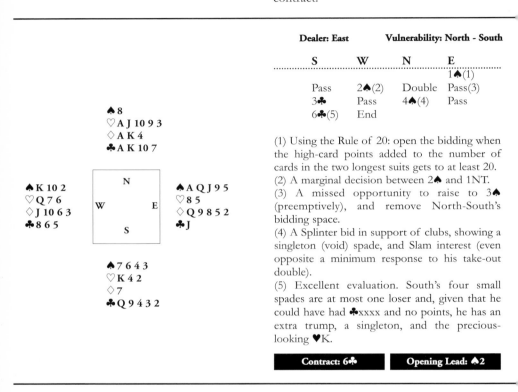

Dealer: East		Vulnerability: North - South	
S	W	N	E
			1♠(1)
Pass	2♠(2)	Double	Pass(3)
3♣	Pass	4♠(4)	Pass
6♣(5)	End		

(1) Using the Rule of 20: open the bidding when the high-card points added to the number of cards in the two longest suits gets to at least 20.
(2) A marginal decision between 2♠ and 1NT.
(3) A missed opportunity to raise to 3♠ (preemptively), and remove North-South's bidding space.
(4) A Splinter bid in support of clubs, showing a singleton (void) spade, and Slam interest (even opposite a minimum response to his take-out double).
(5) Excellent evaluation. South's four small spades are at most one loser and, given that he could have had ♣xxxx and no points, he has an extra trump, a singleton, and the precious-looking ♥K.

Contract: 6♣	Opening Lead: ♠2

West led the two of spades to East's ace. With nothing appealing to switch to, East continued with the queen of spades, dummy trumping. Declarer cashed dummy's ace-king of trumps (East playing the jack on the first round, and then discarding), and, leaving West's last trump out, paused to reflect on the problem of the third round of hearts.

Declarer had a two-way finesse position in hearts. If he thought West held the queen, he would cash the king and play low to the jack. If he thought East held the queen (seemingly more likely as he opened the bidding), he would cash the ace and run the jack. But can you see

that there was no need to take a heart finesse after all?

Declarer crossed to the king of hearts and returned to dummy's ace. No queen had appeared; but both opponents following low to reveal the three-two split in the suit was all that he needed. He cashed the ace-king of diamonds, discarding his third heart (key play), trumped a heart (so it was West who held the queen), crossed to dummy's ten of trumps (drawing West's last trump), then cashed the two established hearts discarding his two losing spades.

Slam made.

Deal 50

Our fiftieth and final deal sees how the Splinter Bid can assist partner in a competitive bidding scenario.

At Table One North might have left in his partner's double of 4♠. However, feeling that he had not fully imparted the playing strength of his hand - especially with his singleton spade - he understandably bid one more.

With South declaring the uncomfortably high contract of Five Hearts, West elected to begin with a passive trump lead (for want of an attractive alternative). Declarer played low from dummy, and won his eight. At Trick Two he led a diamond, and guessed correctly to play dummy's jack. East won the ace, and switched to the five of clubs (best). Declarer played low, in the vain hope that East held the king. West won the king, and cashed the ace of spades. Down one - East-West +100.

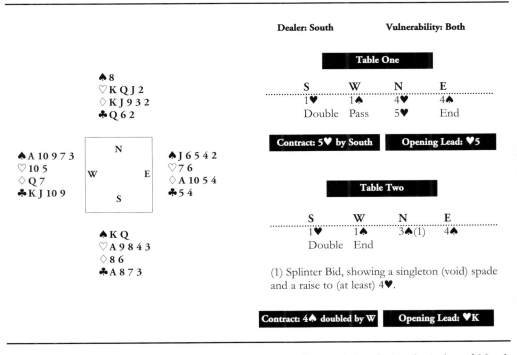

Dealer: South　　　　**Vulnerability: Both**

Table One			
S	W	N	E
1♥	1♠	4♥	4♠
Double	Pass	5♥	End

Contract: 5♥ by South	Opening Lead: ♥5

Table Two			
S	W	N	E
1♥	1♠	3♠(1)	4♠
Double	End		

(1) Splinter Bid, showing a singleton (void) spade and a raise to (at least) 4♥.

Contract: 4♠ doubled by W	Opening Lead: ♥K

At Table Two North felt much more comfortable about passing his partner's double of Four Spades - because he had already shown his hand very precisely with the Splinter Bid. This was the crux.

Defending Four Spades (doubled) by West, North led the king of hearts and, when it held, followed with the queen. South overtook with the ace, and switched to a low club (best). West guessed wrongly by playing the jack, and North won his queen and returned a club to South's ace. Declarer could not avoid losing a trump trick, and the second round of diamonds, so the contract was down three. North-South +800.

A 900 point swing in favour of the North who splintered.